bright child

Dr Richard C. Woolfson

hamlyn

Contents

Language   **84**

Learning   **102**

Social and Emotional Development   **120**

The Importance of Stimulation

Between 2½ and 5 years your child's development moves at an astounding pace, but there is still lots that you can do to help the process along. He needs your stimulation and guidance to boost his confidence, strengthen his learning skills, help him develop relationships with other children his own age, improve his hand–eye coordination and movement skills, and enhance his all-round development. Every day he has many challenges to face and lots of obstacles to overcome. That's part of growing up. Yet your active support, stimulation and encouragement will ensure that he develops into a bright child.

The World is Mine

Your child's zest for getting more involved in life around him drives him every single day. And now that he's 2½ years old his language skills have increased to the point where he can talk in well-formed, appropriate sentences, ask you lots of questions and play a meaningful part in conversations. From listening carefully to the way words are used around him, your growing child's own use of language becomes increasingly sophisticated – by the time he reaches his fifth birthday his interest extends to written as well as spoken language, as he grasps the early stages of reading.

These changes – along with progress in movement, hand–eye coordination, learning and sociability – have two main effects on your child's

development. First, his new skills bring him success because he can achieve much more than he did before. This whets his appetite for further progress, making him want to do even more.

As a crawling baby, for instance, he dreamed of climbing to the top of the stairs to discover the mysteries that lay there, and he struggled in vain to make that difficult climb. Now, however, he cruises the stairs with ease and has new and ambitious

targets, such as kicking a ball hard or running faster than all his friends. In other words, he continually sets new goals for himself as a result of the satisfaction derived from achieving the previous

Below: Free play with friends forms an increasingly important part of your child's activities, boosting his imagination and his communication skills.

ones. His enthusiasm for new experiences is limitless.

The second main impact of his improved developmental skills is that he is able to seek his own stimulation. Compared to his earlier stages, your growing child searches out many more new activities on his own, without relying on you so

Above: The activities you share should be fun – the more pleasure you both get, the more motivated your child will be.

✦✦✦✦ Top·Tips ✦✦✦✦

1. Be spontaneous. Your child learns a lot just by watching and interacting as part of his daily routine – it may perhaps seem dull to you, but it's exciting to your child. Use any learning possibilities that arise naturally, as well those that you plan for him.

2. Have fun. Stimulation in a tense atmosphere isn't fun, either for you or for your child, and he learns less when he is anxious. So ensure that stimulation is a pleasant experience for him. He doesn't have to laugh all the time but he should enjoy himself.

3. Encourage free play. His development is also boosted by having plenty of episodes of free play, in which he chooses what to do. These moments allow him to practise on his own what he has already learned.

4. Praise progress. His enthusiasm for meeting new learning challenges feeds off your delight in his progress. He is intrinsically motivated to advance himself, but the pride he sees on your face gives him a further boost.

5. Enjoy his company. Your child has a unique blend of characteristics, skills and abilities – that's what makes him the wonderful child he is. Your obvious love and pleasure at being with him lifts his confidence in learning.

much. You'll burst with pride as you watch his self-driven determination to learn more. But despite his self-confidence and independence, you can't leave him to his own devices all the time. Motivation will take your child so far – your support, stimulation and guidance can open entirely new horizons for him.

Partners in Progress

Using the suggestions in this book gives you an opportunity to make your child's vital pre-school years more interesting, more rewarding, more challenging... and, of course, more fun. And that's what makes a bright, dynamic child. The aim of stimulation should not be to force his progress artificially in a specific direction; rather, it should be to provide a set of new experiences that harness his innate desire for self-progress.

Think of yourself as your child's 'learning partner'. In other words, his progress depends on the interaction between his unique abilities, your unique personality and his everyday life. Your role is to work with your child, matching stimulation to his current stage of development – not to take over, or to provide so much structure that his natural spontaneity is lost.

Bear in mind that you've been doing this all the time already, right from the moment he was born. It was you who judged when he was ready to move from liquids to solids, when he was capable of tackling the more complicated jigsaw, and when he was able to play on the pedal toy. You have intuitively monitored his development closely, ever ready to enhance his progress to the next stage. The role of your stimulation during this next period of his life remains the same.

Using this Book

When planning a programme of stimulation for your child, there is invariably the possibility that you might focus on one specific area of development while unintentionally neglecting the others. But that is always a mistake. For instance, parents who are so concerned about their child's learning progress that they forget about her ability to mix with others her own age will soon find that she is unhappy. That's why this book offers an all-round perspective that takes into account each aspect of your child's development. When using the suggestions given throughout this book as a source of ideas for stimulating your child, always take a balanced approach.

How to Use this Book

There are many ways in which we can categorize aspects of child development. This book focuses on five main dimensions:

• **movement.** This is your child's ability to move her arms, legs and body in a coordinated and purposeful way. At 2½ years old she has barely mastered the skills of jumping into the air and landing steadily on her feet, whereas by the time she is 5 years old she can hop, run and balance on one foot. Her increased confidence means that she is more adventurous with outdoor play.

• **hand–eye coordination.** The most noticeable change in this area of development is your child's early writing skills. Hand control develops rapidly until she is able to copy her own name onto a piece of paper, and perhaps even to write it herself. Drawing skills also improve, so that her sketches contain more details and the objects in them are easily recognizable. She uses scissors to cut paper.

• **language.** Her use of language becomes much more mature and varied during this stage. With every passing day, she is able to express her ideas more clearly and forcefully to you. Her ability to use

Below: To maximize your child's interest ensure that you provide her with a wide range of toys and activities, both indoors and outdoors.

more complex sentences enables her to take part in conversations with children and adults. She uses language to learn, to voice her feelings and to exchange views with her friends.

• **learning.** It's hard to imagine that this thinking, clever child before you was once a baby who didn't understand how to place a plastic block into the correct hole in the shape-sorter! As she approaches the start of infant school, your child can already count at least up to five, compares objects using a number of different characteristics, and has good concentration when trying to solve a problem facing her.

• **social and emotional.** Friendships now play a large part in her life. During this period her social skills improve – especially her ability to share toys, to cooperate with others during a game and to follow rules. Her independence grows too, as she learns to dress herself, to take responsibility for personal hygiene and to complete elementary household chores.

Every Child is Different

This book provides you with lots of ideas for promoting your child's development, but it is not a checklist that should be worked through in a rigid, inflexible way. Remember that your child is unique, with her own strengths and weaknesses, likes and dislikes, anxieties and fears. What suits one child might not suit another – a

Above: By 4½ your child will have progressed greatly, but all children acquire skills at different rates so don't worry if he takes longer than his friends.

•••• Top•Tips ••••

1. Flexibility. If a planned activity doesn't prove popular with your child, be ready to try something new. There are always several ways to help your child acquire the same skill, so be prepared to try a different approach.

2. Variation is good. Just as you get bored with repeating the same activity over and over again, so does your child. Don't be surprised, therefore, if her eyes glaze over when you bring out the same old jigsaw once again. Provide her with a range of toys.

3. Accept her individuality. You'll find that your child has some of the abilities associated with her age, some associated with older children, and some associated with younger children. This spread of skills is perfectly normal.

4. Be creative. The activities suggested in this book are not exhaustive. You'll be able to think of additions. That's great – create your own set of activities to use in conjunction with those offered here.

5. Stay calm. This book does not provide you with a curriculum for your child that she must pass through at all costs. Sometimes she won't be ready to acquire a skill just yet, so don't make a big fuss. Relax and return to the activity at a later date.

programme of stimulation that benefits your best friend's child might not have the same effect on yours. So use this book as a flexible range of suggestions, some of which will be more appropriate for your child than others.

Bear in mind, too, that all these areas of development are linked to each other. Take hand–eye coordination, for instance. Although this aspect of development is outlined in its own

chapter, the positive effects of progress in hand control aren't restricted to manual tasks. For instance, when your child manages to hold a pencil firmly, she uses this skill to learn to write, which in turn improves her self-esteem, which then gives her the confidence to make new friends.

Your Attitude

Your attitude towards stimulation determines the impact and success of your involvement in your child's development. Push him too hard to achieve the milestones for his age group, spend too much time on a programme of activities designed to promote his skills, get too intense about his achievements – and you'll soon find that his natural enthusiasm for play evaporates. On the other hand, show no interest in your child's progress, spend no time playing with him, have a completely relaxed attitude when it comes to acquiring new skills and you'll soon find that he's lethargic. Try to find a suitable balance.

An Upbeat Approach

Watching your child's development unfold has high points and low points. Sometimes you'll be astounded when he unexpectedly learns something new; at other times, however, you'll feel frustrated when he seems unable to progress at an activity that you assumed he would master with ease. To help you develop a consistently positive, supportive attitude towards stimulating your growing child, ask yourself the following questions:

• **do I think that my child has the potential to progress at a satisfactory rate?** If you don't believe in your child and his abilities and talents, then he won't believe in himself either. It's not about blind faith – rather, it's about your conviction that he is a capable child with the potential to progress in all areas of his development. Any lack of confidence you may have in his abilities will eventually spread to

Right: Listen carefully to what your child tells you – something that may seem trivial to you might be important to her.

your child himself. Your upbeat, positive outlook enables stimulation to have a powerful effect.

• **will I recognize if I over-stimulate him?** You'll very quickly get to know when your child has had enough. For instance, when he is pushed too hard you'll probably find that he becomes tired, irritable and uninterested, or he may lose concentration, or be cheeky to you. Look for these signs that tell you he needs a break. Remember that an exhausted, bored child doesn't learn

anywhere near as well as a refreshed, energetic child.

• **are my expectations of my child realistic?** Of course you want him to achieve, to be capable and to progress swiftly during these vital pre-school years. And of course you'd be delighted if he proves to be more advanced than all his friends. High hopes ensure you set high standards. But if your expectations are unrealistically high, you will set your child up for failure and disappointment. Harmonize

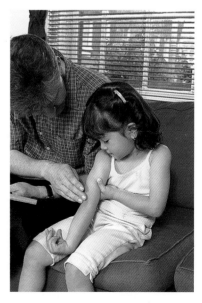

your expectations with his abilities.

• **what do I mean when I say I want a 'bright' child?** In this book, the word 'bright' does not simply mean 'clever'. Developing your child's learning is one aim of some of the activities presented here, but not the sole aim. A truly bright child is one who is dynamic, interested and responsive, and who interacts spontaneously with his surroundings; he is also sociable, contented, has a high level of self-confidence and is comfortable in his relationships with others.

• **am I able to play with my child without taking over completely?** The suggested stimulation activities in this book provide ideas for you to use to enhance your child's play – to extend his normal routine so that he gets more out of it than if he were left to play alone all the time. Make sure that you don't do so much that the activities become yours, not his. Encourage and stimulate your child, while giving him enough time to achieve the solution himself.

• **do I know him well enough to provide activities at just the right level?** Through careful observation of your growing child, you are already aware of his current level of development in the key areas outlined in this book. Use this understanding to choose activities that are slightly ahead of his present point of progress (so that his appetite for these challenges remains high), but not too advanced (so that he gives up because he knows he can't achieve the targets).

Below: Your participation in games will encourage your child and as he gets older you can let him make the rules sometimes.

✦✦✦✦ Top·Tips ✦✦✦✦

1. Avoid comparisons. Continually remind yourself that every child develops at his own pace. There will be times when his development seems either to slow down or to speed up – don't worry about these individual variations.

2. Take a break. You don't have to stimulate your child every minute of every day. He benefits from having plenty of unstructured leisure time, just as you do. It's good for you and your child to have time to relax and do nothing in particular.

3. Resist regimentation. Play should always be fun for your child. If you over-organize his daily activities, his enjoyment will decrease. Aim for a flexible agenda with lots of variety, instead of a fixed formula of stimulation each day.

4. Be spontaneous. Keep in mind that your child's development is boosted by his normal, unplanned everyday experiences, such as playing with water in the bath or studying the products on supermarket shelves. Learning goes on all the time.

5. Talk to others. Many parents like to swap stories about their child's progress – both successes and problems – with friends. This helps them to maintain a balanced outlook. Sharing proud moments as well as your anxieties may be good for you.

Summary of

Development

Nature or Nurture

Now that your child is that bit older, you are aware that she has her own distinctive characteristics. At this stage, you can identify some features in her behaviour that were present at birth and are still present today, and you can also spot aspects of your child today that were not obvious when she was born. You'll probably have formed your own opinion about whether these traits are inherited or are acquired through experience and learning. Bear in mind, however, that your perspective on this 'nature versus nurture' debate affects the way you interact with your growing child.

Opposing Viewpoints

Here are some examples of the ways in which your own attitude towards the different roles of heredity and environment in your child's life can influence her development.

Below: Interest or aptitude for something like music may become apparent early on.

If you believe firmly in the 'nature' argument (namely, that your child's talents are inborn), then it is probable that you:

• don't place much importance on providing stimulation for her because you expect her abilities to develop no matter what happens.

• take a relaxed, fatalistic approach

to her development, on the basis that there is not much you can do to affect it anyway.

• accept her strengths and weaknesses without challenge, and do not feel the need to stretch her abilities in any specific direction.

• assume that all similarities between yourself and your child are

due to inherited characteristics and that this has nothing to do with learned behaviour.

If you strongly support the 'nurture' argument (namely, that your child's abilities are determined by her environment), then you probably:
• regard a well-structured programme of stimulation as the vital key to your child's satisfactory development.
• are ready to get involved with a plan of stimulation whenever you detect any area of her development that could be improved.
• assume that playing with your child and providing challenges for her to tackle is a necessary part of your parental responsibilities.
• think that perceived similarities between you and your child arise through imitation, because she unintentionally copies you.

Fortunately, few parents and professionals take either of these extreme approaches. Common sense and everyday experience tell you that your child's progress isn't as simple as either 'nature' or 'nurture' alone. True, there are many skills which a child shows early on that undoubtedly are innate (such as musical ability), but there are also many skills that improve rapidly just with practice (such as learning to read). It's more a question of how much both influences contribute to her overall development than of its being entirely one or the other.

Maximize Potential

The picture of development is even more complex. The reality is that your child's progress is a dynamic, constantly changing process that is much more than a simple combination of the abilities she was born with and the stimulation she receives as she grows during her early years. For example, every time you respond with excitement when she learns something new or acquires another skill, her confidence and motivation are heightened, which makes her try harder, which in turn makes you even more delighted with her. So your interest, her curiosity, your support, her willingness to take a risk, your guidance when success eludes her, are just some of the many other factors that play a part.

What matters most is that you try to maximize your child's full potential, and that you create an environment at home in which her natural talents are nurtured and extended as much as possible. Of course you will find that there are limits to what she can do, yet you should help her to go as far as she can, whether it's teaching her how to dress herself or helping her to finish that difficult jigsaw puzzle. So get involved, use the activities suggested, and don't be restricted by the nature versus nurture debate.

Above: At around 4 years of age these two boys are learning a great deal by doing some simple planting in pots in the garden.

✦✦✦✦ Top ✦ Tips ✦✦✦✦

1. Play with your child. There is an emotional dimension to development, irrespective of your child's current skills. The fact is that she loves attention from you whatever the time of the day, and this puts her in a positive, enthusiastic frame of mind.

2. Expect variations in rate of progress. You'll find that some months your child leaps forward in her development and yet at other times she appears to make no progress whatsoever. Surges and plateaux in progress like this are normal.

3. Encourage her natural interests. Every child has her own individual tastes when it comes to play activities. Try to identify the toys and games that she particularly enjoys and use these interests as the basis for other activities, too.

4. Don't anticipate even development. The chances are that your child's progress will be uneven. For example, at times her physical development may be further ahead than her learning skills, or her social development may lag behind her language ability.

5. Affect what you can. In the end, you can't do much about your child's inherited characteristics as they are fixed, but you can do plenty about directing these innate skills and providing stimulation to encourage the development of new skills.

Non-Verbal Communication

Now that he is 2½ years old, your child's spoken language is excellent and he expresses his views clearly using words. Yet this doesn't diminish the importance of his non-verbal communication – he continues to convey subtle messages about his feelings and attitudes through body language. It's more sophisticated, varied and complex than in earlier years, so you have to work harder in order to interpret it. Some psychological estimates suggest that when you and your growing child communicate with each other, over half the meaning is transmitted non-verbally through body language. Your child tends to use body language to express his emotions rather than information.

Pay Attention

Another reason why you should learn to understand your child's body language is that he exercises less control over it than he does with spoken language. Think about it for a moment. When your 5-year-old decides to tell you something, he considers it, he chooses his words carefully, and then he tries to talk in a way that he believes will be most effective. In other words, his spoken language is generally well controlled (except, perhaps, when he is upset or in a temper).

But this is not the same with your child's body language. Much of his non-verbal communication is involuntary. For instance, he doesn't

deliberately scratch his ear when he tells you a lie, he just can't help himself; and he doesn't willingly let his shoulders sag and his head droop when he lacks confidence in himself. It's this uncontrolled aspect of non-verbal communication that makes it so exciting, because it

provides you with access to the inner feelings and emotions that your child may not want, or be able, to express in words.

Below: By learning to read your child's body language you will gain a far greater understanding of his or her emotions.

Moments may arise when your child tells you one thing using spoken language but something completely different using his body language – like the time your 3-year-old assured you he wasn't upset by the fight with his best friend, but the next minute his facial expression crumpled and he burst into tears.

✦✦✦✦ Top · Tips ✦✦✦✦

1. Look for groupings. Hand movements, for example, won't tell you as much on their own as they do when combined with facial expression and posture. Look at the whole picture of his body language, not just one element.

2. Practise interpreting. Make a specific point of noticing his body language, which you can only do by looking at him when he speaks to you. The more you do this, the easier it becomes, and you will gradually become more adept at it.

3. Act on your assessment. There's no point interpreting his non-verbal communication unless you intend to do something about it. If you think he is upset, give him a cuddle; if you think he is afraid, give him extra reassurance.

4. Examine your own non-verbal communication. Almost certainly your child's body language is similar to yours. It makes sense, therefore, to become more aware of the range of gestures you use and the underlying feelings associated with them.

5. Watch other children. Look at other children and the ways in which they convey meaning non-verbally. You'll probably see different gestures, ones that are not used by your own child, but this broadens your general understanding of body language.

Other clashes between verbal and non-verbal communication could be more subtle – like the time your 5-year-old insisted he wasn't afraid of visiting the dentist, but you noticed that he nervously rubbed his fingers together in the waiting room. In most instances, non-verbal messages are more genuine than verbal ones precisely because they are less deliberate.

Dimensions of Your Child's Non-Verbal Communication

The various dimensions of non-verbal communication all interact with each other and you should therefore interpret the full range as presented by your child, not just one dimension in isolation. The main features of your child's body language between the ages of 2½ and 5 years are:

• **head position.** The way he holds his head could be upright and facing you, which suggests that he is confident and self-assured; or may be nodding or shaking, which indicates whether or not he agrees with you; or it could even be pushed forward at a rather menacing angle, which lets you know that he's angry about something.

Above: At 3½ this little boy is protecting his bricks with his legs; he regards them as his and signals that they are not for sharing.

• **facial expression.** Look at all aspects of your child's expression including his brow, eyes, mouth, and even his tongue. They all tell you something about his inner feelings. For instance, a relaxed, easy expression with mouth open lets you know that he's contented, while screwed-up facial muscles reveal that he is tense or angry.

• **body distance.** If your child stands close and presses himself against you, the chances are that he feels very insecure, or very afraid, or very angry with you – you'll be able to identify the real emotion by studying other aspects of his body language at the same time, such as hand grip and breathing.

• **body posture**. When he stands facing you square-on, with his hands on his hips, fists clenched and a tight facial expression, you can have no doubt that he is angry about something. Likewise, you know that when he slumps in a chair, legs stretched, arms hanging loosely by his sides and breathing easily, he feels contented.

Night Training

Now that she is 2½ years old, your child's independence takes a huge surge forward. In particular, during this period in her life she becomes ready to gain bowel and bladder control at night. This is because she now has a higher level of self-confidence, is able to move from the bed to the toilet easily without requiring any help from you, already has experience of learning to become dry during the day, and is motivated to achieve this skill because she wants to be like a 'big girl'. Night training, however, rarely goes according to plan, so be prepared for occasional disappointments along the way.

Left: Setbacks may upset your child but if you are patient and approach the situation calmly she will overcome them.

Choosing the Right Time

By the time she reaches her third birthday, your child has probably been reliably dry during the day for a number of months. Memories of changing her nappy several times during the waking hours are in the past. Of course she still has occasional 'accidents', perhaps when she becomes so engrossed in a piece of play that she leaves it too late to reach the toilet in time. These occasional episodes of wetting during the daytime are perfectly normal and become less frequent with each passing month.

Now is a good time to extend your child's bowel and bladder control to night-time, too. Many parents start night training between the ages of 2½ and 3 years, although some leave it even later than that. Choose a time that suits you and your child. Remember that she isn't going to achieve night dryness instantly, so be prepared for mounds of extra washing, particularly when you begin the process.

The best time to begin night training is when your child is ready – there is little point in starting until your child is interested and ready to cooperate with you. There are various signs of readiness that you should look out for. For instance, your child might ask to go without a nappy at night – positive motivation is a great foundation. Or she may take off her nappy in the morning and proudly show you that it is bone dry.

When you have decided to begin toilet training at night, take your child with you to buy trainer pants to wear instead of a night nappy. This gets her involved right from the start. Also buy a plastic mat to go under her sheet, just in case she has any accidents. Explain to her that you hope she'll have a dry bed in the morning when she wakes up and that she shouldn't get upset if the bed is not dry. Make sure she can find her own way to the toilet during the night if she wakes in darkness; you could leave a light on in the hall or on the landing in case this should happen. You could also have a potty in her bedroom, rather than leave her to negotiate the stairs alone in the dark during the night. It makes sense for her to use the toilet just before bedtime.

Some children – even those who became daytime potty trained very quickly – take several months to achieve dryness at night, too. Look on the process as a partnership between you and your child. Statistics suggest that boys take longer than girls to acquire night-time control; around 75 per cent of children achieve this goal by the age of 3 years.

Patience, Patience, Patience
Night training needs a calm atmosphere to work effectively. No child can be coerced into achieving dryness at night: coaxing and support is more appropriate. If you find that your child is wet during the night, calmly put her sheets and pyjamas into the washing machine and tell her that you're sure she'll

have a dry bed tomorrow morning. There is no point in showing irritation with her. Be patient – remember that she is just as keen as you that she wakes up dry.

When she does achieve success – which she will eventually do one morning – give her a big hug and tell her how proud you are of her. It's common for a child to be dry for a couple of nights, then wet, then dry again. Although the unpredictable nature of night training in the first few weeks can be daunting for both parent and child, the pattern will probably stabilize after a month or so.

Below: Some children initially feel insecure with no nappy at night. Reassure and encourage her to see the process as positive.

❖❖❖❖ Top ❖ Tips ❖❖❖❖

1. Establish sensible drinking habits. Although your child's bladder fills when she is asleep whether or not she has a drink just before she climbs into bed, common sense tells you to restrict her fluid intake as bedtime approaches.

2. Talk positively. Always take an upbeat approach, in which you anticipate success rather than failure. Use the terms 'dry' and 'not dry' instead of 'wet', and give your child lots of reassurance that she will be dry tomorrow.

3. Don't wake her during the night. Some parents wake their child before they go to bed themselves, then take her to the toilet. However, this strategy simply means that the parents take responsibility for bladder control, rather than handing it to their child.

4. Persist. It can be demoralizing to be faced with one wet bed after another, morning after morning. But don't put her back into nappies. Once you have made the decision to start night-time training – and assuming she is ready to begin – follow it through until she succeeds.

5. Be philosophical. She'll get there eventually. If your child struggles to achieve bladder control at night, it does not mean there is anything wrong with her or with your training techniques. She is just not ready to master this skill yet.

Encouraging Kindness

Your child has a natural tendency to be kind and caring towards others – you'll already have seen him comfort his tearful friend, perhaps by giving him a cuddly toy to ease his unhappiness. Acts of this sort occur spontaneously during childhood, suggesting that a child has a caring instinct. However, he has other instincts that compete with this, such as the need to satisfy his hunger, and so your 4-year-old might push another child out of the way in order to grab the last biscuit. You can help your child to develop and enhance his caring attitude so that his sensitivity and kindness dominate.

Aspects of Kindness

There are three main aspects to kindness in childhood:

- **cooperation.** This occurs when your child works with another child in order to complete a common activity, such as building a model with construction blocks. Cooperation requires your growing child to think about the other child, to take that child's point of view into account, and to play in synchrony with him – all key characteristics that underlie kindness.

- **sharing.** In the true sense of the word, sharing involves your child giving up something of his own without any guarantee of anything in return. Genuine sharing means that your child is willing to put his personal happiness at risk in order to please someone else. So when your 4-year-old decides to let his best friend play with his favourite jigsaw, he is demonstrating his caring nature.

- **empathy**. Your child shows empathy when he experiences the feelings of someone else. It's quite different from sympathy, which is the feeling of sorrow on seeing another person in distress. For your child to be empathetic, he has to understand the other child's point of view and to feel what that other child feels – for instance, you may find that he cries when he sees his friend cry.

Do your best to encourage these particular attributes in your growing child. He is strongly influenced by the behaviour of those around him. If you

Below: This 5-year-old is mending a skipping rope for a younger child. Praising kindness will encourage further instances.

demonstrate kindness towards him, and if others in your family show that they care about each other, your child is likely to adopt such an attitude as well. Research has also shown that a child who feels loved and valued, and who has a strong emotional connection with his parents, tends to be more caring towards his peers.

◆◆◆◆ Top · Tips ◆◆◆◆

1. Provide opportunities for sharing. When your child is with his friend, make a specific point of giving him a small snack that he has to share (under your supervision). The more opportunities he has to share, the better he becomes at this.

2. Buy him a small pet. Caring for a domestic pet is a very effective way of heightening your child's sense of responsibility towards others. Even a 3-year-old can be allowed to be the one who feeds the goldfish every day.

3. Explain consequences. Your child may not fully grasp the consequences of his behaviour: for instance, that kindness makes people happy or that selfishness upsets them. Point out the effects his actions have on those around him.

4. Play board games. Board games that have more than one player can only be played properly if all the players cooperate, take turns and follow the rules. This is good practice for your child, though it may take him some time to learn these skills.

5. Acknowledge kindness. When you do observe your growing child making a spontaneous caring gesture, perhaps towards his friend or sibling, let him know you are delighted with his behaviour. He warms to your praise.

Toys and Books

There is evidence that the toys your child plays with can have a direct influence on the way he relates to others his own age. Studies have found, for example, that a child who plays with an aggressive-type toy (such as a toy weapon or soldiers) has a higher level of aggression in his play with others for several hours after he has stopped playing with those toys. Likewise, it has been shown that a child is likely to be more caring towards his peers in the hours following play with non-aggressive toys (such as a bat and ball or paramedic toy figures).

Your child's toys, therefore, do make a difference. It's up to you to decide on the extent to which you

Above: Sharing is hard for young children because they are naturally self-centred and still learning to control this instinct.

let this influence your selection of activities, but common sense tells you that a child who is excited and caught up in a fantasy world of aggressive play may be rougher with friends when he is in that frame of mind. An unvaried diet of aggressive toys and games may suppress his innate caring instinct.

You can also encourage your child's kindness by choosing books for him that involve stories with a caring theme. There are plenty of great books for children that tell a story in which the central character helps others who are weaker or unwell. Your impressionable child is affected by these fictitious role models, and it's better for him to want to be like a caring story character than like a selfish one. Read the book first before deciding whether or not it is suitable for your child.

Left: Teaching a child to look after a pet can help her to understand the wider importance of a caring attitude to others.

Shyness

Your child faces many new social experiences between the ages of 2½ and 5 years, such as starting nursery or playgroup, meeting the other children her childminder also looks after, or starting the infant class itself. Each time she meets a set of unfamiliar children and adults, her social confidence is challenged – it's hardly surprising, then, that your child has episodes of temporary shyness during this phase of her life. Fortunately, she draws on the lessons learned from previous social encounters and is able to consolidate and extend her existing social skills to overcome shyness when it arises.

More Confident

Compared to her shy behaviour when she was a toddler, your 3-year-old is much more composed in company. Those earlier moments of sheer social panic when she saw an unfamiliar relative or friend approach are less frequent now. Experience has already taught your child that nothing dreadful is likely to happen in the company of others, and she also has higher self-esteem. This means that when she starts

Below: New situations – like starting at a nursery or school – can be daunting but support will help overcome initial unease.

nursery or playgroup (and similarly when she starts school) she actually looks forward to it. Of course her shyness may return as she approaches the nursery door for the first time, but these feelings will quickly pass. One of the terrific advantages that young children have over adults is that they can make social contact without having to exchange any words at all – they can play together silently, letting conversation come later.

Shyness becomes even less frequent as your child approaches 5 years old. She mixes with other children her own age every day, and this reduces any feelings of shyness she might have. However, her social

confidence remains vulnerable. All it takes is a sudden thought that her shirt isn't the right colour, or the unexpected fear that she won't know what to say to the others, to trigger a wave of shyness. But at this age she recovers quickly, with your help, and continues with her social plans.

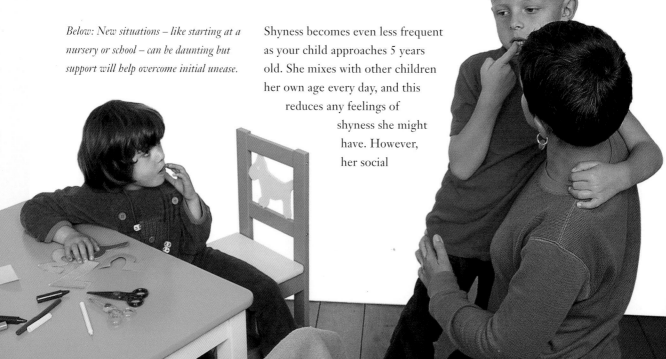

Psychological research has revealed some other facts about shyness at this age:

• around four out of every five adults can remember episodes of shyness when they themselves were pre-schoolers.

• around one-third of all parents describe their 4-year-old as shy, depending on the social circumstances.

• there are huge differences in the degree of shyness experienced. For one child, shyness is momentary; for another, it lasts much longer.

• shyness is more common when children know they have to compete with one another than in situations where cooperation and free play is the norm.

• typically, boys are more shy than girls when they are between the ages of 2½ and 5 years. However, the start of school signals a reversal of this trend.

Take her Seriously

Never belittle your child when she's shy. On the surface, her behaviour may seem silly and irrational – after all, you know she is a wonderful, popular child and that all the others will like her. Your child, though, isn't so sure of herself at that precise moment (hence her shyness). She needs your support, not ridicule.

Watch her closely as she approaches social encounters. You do not want to make her self-conscious, but do look subtly for the tell-tale signs of shyness, such as drooping shoulders,

embarrassment, fidgeting hands, physical closeness to you, complaints of feeling unwell, lack of eye contact or gentle sobbing. Much depends on your child's individual personality. You are probably aware of the indicators of her shyness, so watch out for them.

At these times, simply reassure your child that she'll be fine. Avoid long discussions that delay the moment when she meets the other children. Instead, emphasize how much fun she'll have when she gets there, explain the sorts of activities she will participate in, and keep her moving. Give some practical help, too. For instance, you could help her join a group of other children by going over to them yourself and then gently drawing her in; or you could encourage the other children to come over to you while she stands at your side. She needs you to be strong and supportive when her shyness appears.

Below: Encourage your child to join in group activities that will help boost his confidence.

❖❖❖❖ Top · Tips ❖❖❖❖

1. Give her plenty of opportunities to mix. This is an important age for making friends and for developing her social skills. She should be allowed to play with other children her own age on most days, whether at home, playgroup or nursery.

2. Accept that shyness is normal. Almost every child is shy sometimes, so an occasional loss of social confidence is nothing to worry about. It is not a sign of any underlying emotional problem and it will probably pass very quickly.

3. Arrange for structured activities. Your child may be shy at times when the social situation is not structured, and/or when there is no adult supervision. That's why she might prefer organized leisure classes, with an instructor and a clear purpose to her activities.

4. Don't draw attention to shyness. If you see that your child is shy, try to distract her attention from it, perhaps by pointing out something for her to look at or by introducing a completely new topic of conversation. This might help.

5. Never force shyness away. By all means insist she goes to the party despite her shyness – as long as you also provide advice on how to overcome it – but do this gently and firmly, not harshly.

Making Friends

Friendships matter to your child. Through social relationships, he shares ideas, exchanges information, learns about himself and others, keeps busy, and – perhaps most important of all – has fun. But making friends isn't always easy. Establishing and maintaining relationships with others his own age can be challenging for your child, as it involves lots of social and personal skills, and often hard work. Friendships rarely run smoothly, making it necessary for your child to be able to resolve disagreements with his friends. Spend time helping your child with his friendships – in general, a sociable child is a happy child.

Chop and Change

Your child's friendships change from week to week, and even from day to day. At this age children form friendships for many reasons, most commonly because they like the other child but sometimes because they simply want to play with another child's toy for a few minutes and so become pals with them just for that purpose. Don't be surprised, therefore, when your child tells you that he has a new best friend.

Girls tend to be friends with girls and boys with boys – same-gender friendships generally dominate during the pre-school years, although girls are typically more tolerant of boys than vice versa. Research also shows that a child is usually friendly with someone who is like him in terms of personality, humour and intellect.

Some of the key social skills that help your child to make friends are:
• **pleasant appearance.** Although it's not fair, children do make

Below: At 5 and under friendships are quickly established but may be transitory.

judgements based on first impressions, and this initial assessment can have a long-lasting effect. Your 4-year-old is much more likely to be approached by his peers if he has a smile on his face, looks relaxed, is clean and tidy, and appears contented. A happy appearance makes others feel that he is approachable.

Above: Sharing a joke is an important part of childhood friendships – children will find things hilarious that are lost on adults.

❖❖❖❖ Top ∙ Tips ❖❖❖❖

1. Teach him to use social skills. Your child probably demonstrates many of these basic social skills spontaneously, without any encouragement from you. If not, give him lots of suggestions and then practise these social skills using role play at home.

2. Explain about compromise. Relationships change quickly at this age, often because neither child is ready to give way. Tell your child about compromise, so that he understands that it's possible to reach an agreement that suits both of them.

3. Give him a 'caring' job. He's more likely to form friendships when he has a caring attitude. One way to develop this is by giving him a task at home that benefits others, such as setting the cutlery on the dinner table for everyone.

4. Talk to him about friendships. Chat to your child about his pals, and encourage him to think about why he likes his best friend. This helps him to identify the characteristics he looks for in a friend and makes him more aware.

5. Encourage particular friendships. It's difficult to influence his choice of friends – he'll make his own decisions. However, if there is a child you think would make a good friend for yours, suggest that they play together.

• **self-confidence.** Body language helps to create an air of confidence and friendliness. For instance, encourage your child to look at the other children, stand beside them and hold his head up when alongside them. You'll also boost his confidence by telling him how much the other children will want to play with him and to talk to him.

• **manners.** Of course children aren't bothered about the finer points of social etiquette, but they won't be keen to play beside another child who constantly makes rude noises, pushes his way in front of others, refuses to share his toys and makes insensitive remarks about other children. Good personal hygiene also matters.

Social Language

Friendships are mainly formed – and kept – through spoken language. By the time children are 3 or 4 years old, they chat constantly to each other when playing. Your child will get on better with others when he is prepared to make 'small talk' (by asking, for instance, 'What is your favourite game?') rather than sitting in total silence. And once the introductory stage of friendship is over, it is through words that

emotions are expressed, ideas are exchanged and fights are resolved.

Encourage your child to be chatty, to talk to the other children instead of sitting quietly without saying a word to anyone. He doesn't need to be the funniest child ever, or the most adept with words – he just needs to make a remark every now and then to the others. Spoken language oils the wheels of children's social relationships.

Many childhood friendships break up simply because the children are unable to resolve petty bickering. Rather than say what he feels, a child in this age group is more likely to act on his feelings – that's why he snatches the toy from the other child instead of asking for it. Encourage your child to voice his thoughts , and to resist the temptation to act without explaining himself first. In addition, explain that he needs to be a good listener in order to give his friend a chance to say what he feels, as this cements a friendship and makes it less likely to break up.

Sibling Rivalry

It is likely that by now you have a second child too, and sibling rivalry (that is, jealousy between children in the same family) is therefore a strong possibility. There are two peak periods for sibling rivalry. The first is on the arrival of the new baby, which often unsettles the older child temporarily. The second surge usually occurs when the younger child reaches the toddler stage, because that's when he starts to have practical effects on the life of the older sibling – for instance, when he takes her toys without asking, or tags along uninvited beside her.

Identity

Sibling rivalry between your children is normal – it is extremely common and is not a sign that there is something wrong. Fortunately, there's lots you can do. Don't simply sit back and let your children sort it out – that just won't happen.

Basic practical techniques such as giving each of your children time with you on their own, making each one feel special, showing an interest in their individual lives and avoiding comparisons all help to reduce potential tensions. Yet you need to

do more than that. Bear in mind that sibling rivalry occurs not just because your time, attention and resources are limited, but also because each child has a psychological need to develop his or her own unique identity.

Your 5-year-old, for instance, has her own set of friends and they play their own types of games with their own set of toys. She also has her own taste in music, her own preferences in books and stories, and particular television programmes that she favours. The

presence of her 2-year-old brother can make her feel threatened – she may adore him, but she doesn't want him to get his hands on her toys, look at her books or play with her friends, because that dilutes her personal identity. That's why you hear the complaint 'Tell him to stop touching my things'.

Of course, you need to encourage your children to share, to have a caring relationship and to take responsibility for each other. Yet they should be allowed to establish themselves as unique individuals. In practice, this means recognizing that your children don't have to do the same, play the same or like the same. Although life would be a lot easier for you if they went everywhere together, that's an unrealistic expectation. Your children are less likely to resent one another when they feel secure in their own identity.

Left: Once a younger sibling is mobile and can interfere in an older child's activities, tensions may occur and you will need to judge how long they can spend together.

Sorting Out the Fights

Constant daily arguments between your children wear you down. If their disagreements are regular and intense, you'll be tempted to separate them, with a warning that you won't let them play together until they play properly. There is little chance that they will learn to resolve their disagreements, however, when each is alone in their bedroom. They need your help to learn conflict-resolution skills.

When they do fight, give them a minute or two before getting involved – you may find that when they are left alone with each other the argument is actually resolved. If, instead, the bickering just gets worse, intervene calmly, sit each child down in a chair so that they face each other, do your best to settle them until they are both silent, then ask one of the children (the one who wasn't first the last time you did this) to express her point of view. Make sure the other looks and listens while she talks. When she has finished, give your other child a turn to speak.

Once both points of view have been fully expressed, help them to reach a resolution of their argument and then let them return to play. This is time well spent, as eventually your children will be able to settle more and more of their differences without relying on you to sort things out for them.

Below: A younger sibling learns a lot from older children and they, in turn, learn to share with and help the younger ones.

Starting Nursery

When your child reaches the age of 3 years – or possibly even sooner – you'll probably consider a placement in nursery for him. As well as giving you time to resume your career, a nursery placement provides an array of activities and experiences that supplement the stimulation you provide for your child at home. In addition, he meets new children and learns how to mix with others. Despite all these advantages for promoting his development, starting nursery is a huge step in his life (and also in yours). He needs your help to ensure that he gets off on the right footing.

Choosing the Nursery

There will probably be several nurseries in your area, all meeting the needs of children under the age of 5 in their own way. Find out as much as you can about these by reading their brochures and by asking other parents. Listening to

Below: A good nursery should have a wide range of stimulating activities tailored to the different age groups it caters for.

parents whose children actually attend these nurseries is perhaps the best source of external advice. Then visit each one yourself.

Contact the head of the nursery and arrange a time when the place is full of children, not when they have all gone home. Don't take your child with you on these visits, as he'll distract you and he may like a nursery that you don't. Consider the following points when choosing a nursery for your child:

• **practical arrangements.** There is no point in selecting a nursery whose hours don't suit your own timetable, or that is too difficult to get to, or that does not offer the children lunch when you work at that time. Make sure the organization of the nursery suits you.

• **staffing quality.** Ask about the qualifications of the nursery staff and their experience. You can also enquire about the regularity of staff training. Since your child will spend a considerable amount of time under the care and supervision of these adults, you should be satisfied with their professional standards.

• **nursery building.** A clean, new, freshly painted building doesn't guarantee that the children in it are happy. Yet there is plenty of evidence that children respond best when their immediate surroundings are bright, fresh and well maintained. Have a good look around the entire nursery, including the toilets and playground.

• **nursery activities.** There should be a clear programme for the different age groups. Get an outline of the typical week your child would have at the nursery, in order to find out about the range of activities. Watch how the staff and children interact, and look at the children's work on the walls. The noticeboards carry useful information, too.

Once all your visits are over, and you have considered all the pros and

Top Tips

1. Stay relaxed. You'll probably be tense at the thought of leaving your precious child to cope on his own without you at the nursery. Hide any negative feelings you may have from him, however, or he'll become upset too. Be positive with him.

2. Expect tears. Many children cry when their parent leaves them at nursery for the first time, through a combination of excitement, anxiety and lack of experience. Tears on parting at nursery are common, but he will settle soon after you leave.

3. Keep the separation brief. If your child is upset as you are about to leave, don't stretch out the moment of leaving – that would only make him more upset. Instead, cuddle him, reassure him again and then depart from the nursery.

4. Chat to him about his nursery day. On the way home after collecting your child, chat to him about the other children there, the friends he made and the range of activities he enjoyed. Your interest sharpens his enthusiasm.

5. Get progress reports from staff. Talk to the staff regularly, especially in the early weeks, to find out about your child's progress and any minor problems that he experiences. (Do this when he starts school, too.)

Above: Talking to your child about what she has done at nursery will give her a sense of pride in her day's achievements.

cons, make your choice. Tell your child about the selected nursery, without telling him about the others you also considered. Speak positively about it and mention the names of any children there whom he already knows.

Making a Start

Arrange for you and your child to visit the nursery together for an hour, preferably a week before he actually starts there. Stay in the nursery room with him during that visit. When it's over, talk to him about all the marvellous things he saw and did there. This ensures his enthusiasm for the first day.

When that day arrives, stay calm even though you may feel a little upset yourself. Explain to your child that you will settle him in (and probably stay in the nursery for part of that session) to ensure that he is comfortable there, and then you'll leave him and collect him later. Emphasize that he will thoroughly enjoy himself, that the other children will like him, that the staff are terrific, and that you'll see him very soon. When the time comes for you to leave him there for the first time, give him a quick cuddle, a word of reassurance and then leave. Rest assured, he'll be fine.

Gender Differences

Major gender differences in behaviour, clothes and play patterns emerge during the pre-school years. By the time she's 5 years old your child also has fixed views about 'boyness' and 'girlness'. The development of her gender identity is due partly to biological influences (boys have a higher level of testosterone, a hormone linked to aggressiveness), partly to social influences (she watches the reactions of others towards boys and girls), partly to media influences (the way boys and girls are portrayed in film and television affects her) and is partly learned from you (your attitudes to gender have a direct impact on your child).

Facts about Gender

Compared to boys, girls are better at cooperating and sharing, argue less frequently, are far less likely to resort to violence, and are more likely to conform to limits set by their parents. In addition, girls like to play with girls and boys like to play with boys – occasionally there are opposite-gender friendships, but these are in the minority. Some other ways in which your child expresses her gender identity include:

Left and right: Girls and boys naturally split into gender groups. These 3-year-old girls are dancing together while the little boy is standing on the sidelines.

• **what she wears.** The current trend towards wearing unisex sports-type clothes has reduced the clothing gap between boys and girls. However, you will still find that girls prefer yellow, pink and light blue, whereas boys typically like to wear dark colours such as black, dark blue or deep red.

• **the games she plays.** If you have an opportunity to watch boys and girls play, it won't take you long to realize that boys like up-and-at-'em action games with lots of boisterous physical contact and plenty of noise, while girls prefer more gentle, quieter activities that involve following rules and turn-taking.

• **self-help.** Girls generally learn self-help skills at an earlier age than boys, and are more willing to put these into practice. Statistics show that girls are usually

potty trained earlier than boys, can dress themselves at an earlier age and are willing to help with household chores earlier as well.

• **sensitivity.** By the age of 4 or 5 years, boys are less able to express their feelings verbally than girls, and are more likely to remain silent than to speak about whatever troubles them. By the time they start school, girls are way ahead in terms of language skills.

• **group behaviour.** Studies have found that girls tend to behave differently as soon as boys appear in the same room. For instance, they become less outgoing, talk in quieter voices and narrow the distance between themselves so that they are closer to each other.

Breaking the Barriers

Although these gender differences and stereotypical views on gender develop early in childhood, the fact is that there is no good reason why a girl should not play football or a boy should not play with a doll. Of course, others might look disapprovingly at such unexpected behaviour, but that is simply an expression of their own fixed views. Your child should be allowed free choice in play and should not be limited by gender barriers.

In fact, breaking these barriers could be good for her. Since play is crucial to your child's development, it stands to reason that the more varied her play experiences, the more likely she is to enhance her development. If she is able to play with toys and activities traditionally associated with boys, she simply broadens her experience. Diversity is good for your growing child, girl or boy.

Some parents describe their daughter as a 'tomboy' because she likes to wear clothes normally associated with boys. Again, this is simply a matter of personal preference. Maybe she wants to dress like that because she thinks boys' clothes are more comfortable or more colourful, or perhaps she just wants to be different from all her friends. Whatever the reason for her clothes preference, it won't do her any harm.

Below: Children benefit from expressing their personalities through play, and to choose what and whom they play with.

✦✦✦✦ Top ∙ Tips ✦✦✦✦

1. **Encourage individuality.** Try not to be limited by society's views on gender. Let your child play with a toy even though it's normally for boys, if that's what she wants. She is entitled to express her individuality through toys, games and clothes.

2. **Talk with your child.** Both boys and girls benefit from being able to use words to express their feelings to someone else. If your child finds this difficult, have plenty of discussions with her so that she becomes used to chatting with you.

3. **Don't fuss over gender issues.** The moment your child realizes that you are concerned about her choice of clothes or toys, she'll probably use this as a means of grabbing your attention. Try to adopt a relaxed approach.

4. **Avoid confrontations.** There is no reason to battle with your child because she likes to play football (or he is fascinated by his sister's doll's house). This is a normal extension of her interest in a variety of toys.

5. **Provide a good role model.** Since your child is strongly influenced by your own attitudes and behaviour, try to ensure that in your family home chores are not allocated on a gender basis. This broadens her perspective.

Getting Ready for School

The first day of school approaches very quickly, and before you know it your child is about to wave goodbye to you and enter the infant classroom for the first time. This is a big moment for him (as he starts on this exciting new venture) and for you (as you watch your child take a leap forward in his independence). If your child is well prepared for becoming a pupil, he'll have a great start to school – if he's not, then he may have difficulty settling in. That's why it's important to think ahead about this major transition in your child's life.

Personality, not Intellect

Your child's success in the early days of starting school does not depend on how good he is at reading, counting, writing and spelling – teachers expect to teach children these skills. It's personal traits that really matter. Some of the key attributes to encourage in your child long before he actually starts school are:

• **strong motivation.** A teacher can't force your child to learn – he must want to learn. Ensure that his innate thirst for knowledge remains strong, for instance by taking him to the library, being enthusiastic yourself when you see him learn new things and stimulating his learning skills.

Below: If your child has already developed basic social skills he will find it easier to mix with other children in the playground.

• **self-belief.** He'll learn more in the classroom, and at a faster pace, when he believes in himself as a learner. In other words, his self-confidence affects his school progress. Give him lots of stimulation to develop his learning skills (as outlined in this book) and praise him when he has successes.

◆◆◆◆ Top · Tips ◆◆◆◆

1. Meet some of his future classmates. You probably know some of the children who will be in your child's class at school – he may even play with them at nursery already. Having this social contact helps to reduce his potential anxiety.

2. Involve him in school-related purchases. His enthusiasm for school remains high when he is allowed to express his view about the choice of school bag, pencil case and crayons. He likes to make these choices for himself.

3. Talk positively about school. Whether or not you have pleasant memories of your own school days, talk positively about school to your child. Your bright outlook rubs off on him – discourage doom and gloom tales from older siblings.

4. Visit the school. Take advantage of the school pre-entrance visiting days for prospective pupils. This allows your child to meet his teacher and the rest of the staff, plus the other pupils, and also gives him a chance to look around the entire school building.

5. Allow plenty of time. Avoid rushing your child in the morning – if you are stressed he will be, too. Instead, make sure you know what is needed each day (for instance, PE equipment) and prepare it the night before.

• **listening skills.** For much of the time in the classroom your child listens, sometimes to information and instructions for the whole class, sometimes to instructions just for his group or even for him alone. He also needs to listen to other pupils who share their ideas with him when they work cooperatively.

• **friendliness.** Getting on with his classmates in the classroom and in the playground is extremely important for your child. Aside from playing with his peers every day, he also learns with them in small and large groups. He is required to mix with others, to avoid unnecessary arguments and to share ideas with them.

Independence

Another key quality that affects your child's start to school is his level of independence. Of course he is under supervision at all times from the school staff, but there are lots of everyday challenges he is expected to manage on his own, and you can help him to develop these skills before he becomes a school pupil by practising them with him at home:

• **dressing.** When he starts school, your child should be able to take his jacket on and off, hang it on a designated peg, and take his shoes on and off without any help. Make it easier for him by choosing items that have simple fastenings. For instance, avoid shoes with traditional shoelaces until he's at least 6 or 7 years old.

Right: Make sure your child can take her coat and shoes off and put them on before she starts school – practise this if necessary.

• **toilet.** He'll use the school toilets several times each day, so he needs to be able to attend to his toileting needs independently. These include knowing when to use the toilet, managing to pull his pants and trousers down and back up again tidily, and washing and drying his hands afterwards.

• **eating.** When lunching at school, your child has to be able to make a reasonable choice from the foods available, to place this along with cutlery on his tray, and to carry it to a seat at a table. Good eating habits help him retain popularity with his classmates – nobody wants to sit beside a messy eater.

• **structure.** He'll settle into school if he can adapt to the structure of the typical school day. For instance, he should separate easily from you each morning, be able to find his way around the school building, and be tuned in to the classroom routine so that he knows what to do.

Problems at School

Every parent wants their child to do well at school, to fulfil her potential, to enjoy attending and to like the other pupils and the teachers. And in most instances, that's exactly what happens – the majority of young pupils love school. For some children, however, minor problems occur in the first few months of school which upset them and interfere with their potential progress. Remember that school staff are there not just to teach subjects to your child but also to help her settle in. With the combined efforts of everyone involved, most small challenges facing your child can be resolved quickly.

Minor Hurdles

There are lots of reasons why your child might not feel comfortable in school, ranging from learning difficulties to uncertainty about the location of the school toilet – you'd be surprised at the minor challenges that can completely pre-occupy the mind of your child. Often you have no idea that something troubles her until perhaps she comes home from school in tears, or maybe one day she tells you that she doesn't want to go to school again.

Always take these complaints seriously: if your child works up the courage to tell you, then it must be important to her. See what you can do to help – if you don't support her through this, the chances are that nobody else will. Your child depends on your help at this stage. Typical problems that occur early on in a child's schooling include:

• **school-based difficulties.** Your child might not be able to find her way around the school building for instance, or she may not like the smell in the dining area. She might be reluctant to use the toilet because there's not enough privacy.

• **class-based difficulties.** The noise in the classroom unsettles some children at first. If the teacher speaks in a loud voice and is sharp with the pupils, your child may become anxious. Changes in class routine can also unsettle her.

• **friendship-based difficulties.** She wants to have lots of friends. Small arguments with her new pals, or even feeling left out by others, can cause distress. She likes to feel she is part of the crowd.

• **learning-based difficulties.** Coping with the educational demands of school can be overwhelming for some children. Classroom activities require a level of concentration, effort

Right: At school your child will need to concentrate hard and for longer than before which may take getting used to.

and understanding that she may not be used to.

• **home-based difficulties.** A child can become unsettled at school if she thinks, for example, that her

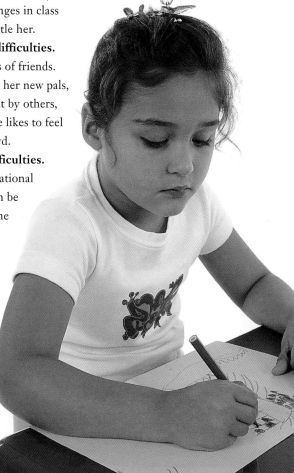

parents are at home giving attention to the new baby. Fights between parents in the house can also make a child feel insecure at school.

You'll probably realize that your child is unhappy at school without having to wait for her to tell you herself. Monitor her progress carefully, especially in the early stages, and talk to her each day about what happened at school. It is important to keep a close dialogue going between the two of you so that you can help her to overcome any problems before they become magnified.

Look out for any signs of distress, such as lack of interest in school, loss of appetite, a poor sleeping pattern, tears when she comes home, reluctance to talk about classroom activities when previously she was very enthusiastic and communicative, and lack of friends. Sometimes an emotional difficulty manifests itself as a physical problem. True, if your child tells you she has a sore tummy, this could be a genuine physical complaint. Should it persist, however, and your family doctor cannot find anything medically wrong with her, the chances are that her discomfort is psychological in nature.

Deal with any concerns as soon as they arise – the sooner the better. Check out all possible reasons for your child's unhappiness at school. There has to be some explanation for her anxiety. Make an appointment with the class teacher and then discuss it fully with him or her. Any problem facing your child is more likely to be resolved when you and the teacher work together in partnership.

Below: If your child is unhappy at school try to find the cause and help to resolve it as quickly as possible.

❖❖❖❖ Top ❖ Tips ❖❖❖❖

1. Be optimistic. Most difficulties that trouble your child at the start will be minor and won't take much to be solved. Your bright, cheery approach – even if you are inwardly anxious – fills her with confidence and this helps her as well.

2. Reassure your child. Let your child know that you recognize that she is worried. Then reassure her that the problem can be solved. Tell her what you intend to do so that she is aware of your plan of action.

3. Maintain good attendance. She should attend school every single day, no matter how troubled she is about going there (assuming she is not ill, of course). Talk to her teacher about your worries and agree a strategy for dealing with her difficulty.

4. Check it out. Whatever practical solution you reach – for instance, to change her grouping in class or to let her take her own lunch instead of buying school food – implement it. Then evaluate it every few days to see whether or not this works.

5. Talk to other parents. It's likely that your child is not the first pupil to have faced this particular difficulty. You may benefit from listening to advice from other parents whose children have had a similar experience.

Special Needs

Up to 20 per cent of children have difficulties with their development. Sometimes these difficulties are minor and are easily overcome by extra stimulation for a short period. In a small minority of children, however, the developmental problems are long lasting, causing them to have long-term special needs. For instance, a child could have persistent slow speech development and not be able to talk in phrases when others his own age already use sentences, or perhaps he experiences difficulty when trying to learn new concepts such as colour names. A child with special needs typically requires extra help once he starts school.

Individual Progress

If your child does have significant difficulties with his development, they were probably identified when he was younger. Most major conditions resulting in special needs

Below: All children – not just those who have special needs – will benefit greatly from socializing with as wide a range of other children as possible.

– such as cerebral palsy, spina bifida, Down's Syndrome and severe learning difficulties – are spotted during a baby's first year. Yet other developmental difficulties may not become apparent until your child is between 2½ and 5 years old, because that is the time when new skills are expected to emerge. Speech and language problems, for instance, are often not regarded by professionals

as serious until a child is around 3 years old. Hearing difficulties might not be accurately pinpointed until this age as well.

Concerns about your child's progress should be addressed now. Speak to your family doctor, who will advise you on suitable specialist assessment. Whatever the nature of the problem, always bear in mind

that your child is the same as he was before the assessment. He has not changed in any way as a result of his difficulty being identified – he's still the same wonderful, unique individual with his own range of characteristics and abilities. The challenge facing you is to ensure

that he receives stimulation to achieve his maximum potential.

A child with special needs will be offered a range of services, all aimed at promoting his development. Much depends on the individual child and the nature of his difficulties, but the type of professional support offered could be speech therapy, physiotherapy, a play programme, or even extra nursery classes. Take advantage of any help like this, as it all benefits your child.

In addition, provide lots of stimulation for him at home. Virtually all the activities presented in this book are just as suitable for your child with special needs, though they might need to be adapted occasionally and your child may need extra encouragement. He has special needs, but like any other child he also has the basic need to be loved, valued and cared for, to experience success and to have his abilities stretched to the limit.

Special Needs at School

Every infant classroom includes children with a wide range of abilities. Don't assume, therefore, that all the other children are brilliant and yours is the only one who struggles with some aspects of

Above: Finding the right learning environment for your child will ensure that he is able to reach his full potential.

the curriculum. The best help you can give is to ensure that the school – and the class teacher in particular – has all the necessary information about your child's difficulties and his associated special needs.

There are several possible support strategies suitable for a child with special needs in school. For instance, a child with physical difficulties could be allowed to leave the class a few minutes ahead of his classmates so that he doesn't have to fight his way through a crowd; a child with visual difficulties can be seated closer to the front of the class and have printed material enlarged; a child with learning difficulties might need instructions explained several times before he fully understands. Sometimes one-to-one teaching for part of the day is appropriate.

It all depends on the individual child. Additional help given to a child with special needs ensures that he thrives in the classroom despite his difficulties. Irrespective of the help your child with special needs requires, try to liaise closely with his teacher.

Development

Movement

- Can jump a short distance into the air from a standing position and land on both feet without falling over.
- Carries out more than one physical task at the same time through improved coordination.
- Is able to hold a toy wheelbarrow firmly in both hands and push it around the room or in the garden.
- Increased physical skills mean she enjoys playing on large outdoor apparatus such as a climbing frame or slide.
- Loves running around in the park with other children or while you watch.
- Enjoys games in which she tries to copy your physical actions, such as standing on one leg.

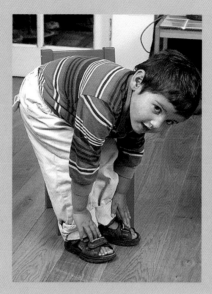 

Hand–Eye Coordination

- Helps you around the house, and tries to dust smooth surfaces, put toys back into the toy box or set cutlery on the table.
- Finds holding and using scissors difficult, but enjoys using them to cut paper.
- Can draw pictures which are often recognizable – you can probably work out what she has tried to sketch.
- Still needs help with personal hygiene tasks such as washing her hands or undressing and dressing herself in the toilet, but is keen to try.
- Copies shapes, such as a plain circle, on a piece of paper. It won't be perfectly round and the ends may not connect.

- Enjoys tearing and crumpling bits of paper and then gluing them onto sheets of paper to make 'pictures'.

Language

- Uses hundreds of different words – perhaps even more than a thousand – in her everyday speech, and combines them into sentences.
- Discovers that questions (mainly 'Who?' and 'Where?') are a good way to get your attention and also to gather information.
- Ceases to use 'baby' speech, and starts to use pronouns such as 'I' and 'he' appropriately and consistently.

- Wants to talk to you all the time about anything that crosses her mind; enjoys conversations and understands that these involve taking turns to speak.
- Thoroughly enjoys performing action rhymes, as these combine her language, memory and coordination skills.
- Can complete the lines of familiar rhymes and poems if you say them to her, leaving her to fill in the last word each time.

2½–3 Year Skills

Learning

- Begins to understand that money is used to buy items, although she doesn't fully understand about different values.
- Her ability to compare two objects using one characteristic emerges, although she gets confused at times. She can't yet compare using two characteristics at the same time.
- Classification skills improve, especially if she has lots of practice at sorting games.
- Is able to respond to basic instructions with only one piece of information, such as 'Bring me the book'.
- Improved memory enables her to recall experiences that occurred recently and also those that took place months ago.
- Can make up her own short stories.

Social and Emotional

- Tries to be more independent, especially with control of her bowel and bladder during the day.
- Still has raging temper tantrums occasionally, when she seems to lose all control, but these become less frequent towards the end of her third year.
- Enjoys the company of other children and wants to spend time with them; at times they bicker with each other. May also experience episodes of shyness.
- May still have difficulty with sharing; may prefer to cling tenaciously to her toys than to let anyone else have them.
- Begins to learn to take turns.
- Can take responsibility for small household tasks, such as putting her toys in the toy box before bedtime.

Development

Movement

- Can propel a pedal toy such as a tricycle slowly along an even surface.
- Balance and coordination are more mature, giving him more confidence when it comes to walking fast and running.
- Copes with walking up small slopes.
- Can jump from the second stair to the ground, with both feet together, when he has seen you do this.
- Stands on his tiptoes for several seconds without putting his heels on the ground, and also walks forward on his tiptoes.
- Enjoys dancing to music, twisting his body and shaking his arms and legs more or less in time to the beat.
- Climbs into his chair at mealtimes and twists his body to get comfortable.

Hand–Eye Coordination

- Holds small objects with a steady hand and moves them without dropping them from his grasp.
- Uses a pile of wooden blocks to build a mini-tower of eight or nine blocks before it eventually topples over.
- Manages to grip scissors firmly in his hand so that he can cut through a large piece of paper.
- Uses a small rolling pin to roll modelling clay, then mashes it up to start again.
- Can unfasten large buttons (the larger, the better) by using his fingers to open the buttonholes.
- Can hold his toothbrush correctly if you show him how, and clean his teeth after a fashion.

Language

- Loves listening to stories and becomes more involved, perhaps discussing it with you as you read to him, trying to turn the pages and pointing to the pictures.
- No longer uses the minimum amount of words to convey meaning but instead uses a string of four or five words.
- Begins to use prepositions.

- Uses adjectives to describe everyday objects or people in his life; at this stage he only uses two or three regularly.
- Can understand and carry out verbal instructions that contain up to three pieces of information.
- Enjoys songs even more now that he is able to learn and remember the words.

3–3½ Year Skills

Learning

- Develops an elementary understanding of numbers because he hears and sees other people using them.
- Demonstrates his increased intellectual maturity through drawing, though his picture of you shows the head extremely large, with no body attached to it and legs sticking straight out from underneath.
- Short-term memory advances to the extent that he may be able to hold new information for a few seconds and then report it accurately back to you.
- May be able to recite the first few numbers in the correct order, though can easily become confused.
- Understands rules of behaviour and the reasons behind them if these are explained clearly to him.
- May confuse coincidence with cause and effect, linking two events that are not in fact connected.

Social and Emotional

- Feels more confident in social situations as a result of mixing with other children and adults, and is more at ease in company.
- Is still emotionally vulnerable, and cries easily over minor upsets.
- Finds it easier to make new friendships; likes to chat to you about his friends and wants you to like them, too.
- Understands the social dimension of eating and wants to be independent at the table, just like the others in his family.
- May have achieved bowel and bladder control at night.
- Enjoys having a small pet, such as a hamster, to care for (with your help and supervision).

Development
Movement

- Has enough confidence to try out all the items in the outdoor play area, including climbing onto a swing and reaching much closer to the top of the climbing frame.
- Enjoys bouncing on a trampoline or bouncy castle.
- Can walk upstairs and downstairs putting one foot on each step at a time, using the banister or wall for support.
- Likes to kick a ball along the ground or pick it up and throw it; catching remains more of a challenge for her.
- Copies you to hop for one or two paces if she concentrates and doesn't go too high.
- Combines physical tasks that each require concentration, such as carrying an object while negotiating the stairs.

Hand–Eye Coordination

- Is able to copy accurately many of the lines that make up written letters, but can't yet form complete letters.
- Can hold a piece of cutlery in each hand, and can drink from a cup.
- Enjoys mixing ingredients with a wooden spoon, rolling the mixture flat, cutting out shapes and putting these into the oven.
- Loves challenging activities that involve hand–eye coordination, such as small jigsaws, and tries hard to achieve success.
- Can find and collect specific items from supermarket shelves by combining her visual skills and hand–eye coordination.
- Threads wooden beads or bobbins (that have a hole drilled through them) onto a thick lace that has a metal tip.

Language

- Humour emerges, much of it revolving around language, reflecting her ability to go beyond a literal understanding of the spoken word.
- Realizes that language can be used to improve her learning and starts to ask 'How?' and 'Why?' questions.
- Increases the length of sentences by using 'and' as a link, but often makes sentences uncomfortably long for the listener.
- May be able to match words of only two or three letters that are printed clearly on individual cards.
- Grasps basic language rules, such as plurals and verb tenses, and uses them in her everyday speech.

3½–4 Year Skills

Learning

- Improved short-term memory allows her to memorize a short poem or telephone number through repetition.
- Concentration increases, so that she plays at one activity or watches a television programme for several minutes before her attention wanders.
- Her organizational skills improve, enabling her to make a more systematic search for something for which she is looking.
- Uses her imagination to create an image that isn't actually in front of her, and is able to tell you details about what she sees.
- Learns discovery strategies and problem-solving skills by watching other children.

- Reaches the first stage of genuine counting – for example, she counts a row of small blocks up to the second or third block and makes an attempt to count on her fingers.

Social and Emotional

- Knows that it is wrong to tell a lie, although she still probably denies her misbehaviour even when you catch her red-handed.
- Becomes upset when she sees one of her friends cry, and tries to comfort the distressed child and cheer her up.
- May react aggressively (physically or verbally) when conflict arises with a friend or family member.
- Dressing skills have improved to the extent that she makes a good attempt to put on her clothes in the morning without help, although she sometimes gets things mixed up.
- May still show extreme shyness when faced with a daunting social situation, such as a party.

- Has a better understanding of the social rules when playing with her friends – for example, she is more able to share her toys, take turns in a game and follow rules.

Development
Movement

- Tries hard to do his best when taking part in simple team games, such as relay races.
- Begins to be able to propel the garden swing himself.
- Hops perhaps three or four paces while still retaining balance, before putting both feet back on the ground.
- Can walk several paces accurately along a straight chalk line, as long as he maintains good concentration.
- Makes an attempt at using a skipping rope, but finds this very challenging.
- May succeed at hitting a soft ball with a large bat or racket.
- Maintains a good steady running speed while still managing to swerve in order to avoid obstacles in his path.

Hand–Eye Coordination

- Likes to wash his hands and face, dress and feed himself independently, though he still needs your help and supervision.
- Can hold a pencil properly if shown how, and makes a good attempt at writing his name, as long as he has a written example to copy.
- Enjoys activities involving hand–eye coordination, such as clearing up dishes after a meal or picking up small items from the floor when tidying up.
- Can stack his toys and games neatly in the cupboard after tidying up, which helps to develop his organizational skills.
- Manipulates modelling clay into many different shapes, using his fingers to

mould it instead of simply shaping it with pressure from his hands.
- Still enjoys water play, and can now pour from one container to another without spilling anything.

Language

- Chats freely to other children at every opportunity and likes to voice his opinion.
- Gives you a reasonably accurate account of a recent experience, perhaps something that happened to him in nursery earlier that day or a video or television programme he watched.
- Uses language to talk to you in some detail about his friends; he tells you why he likes playing with them.

- Probably knows the names of the primary colours and is able to identify them accurately, either as a matching activity or in response to a question.
- Likes to recite familiar rhymes and poems to you, and joins in with songs whenever possible.
- May be able to play 'I spy' using the sounds rather than the names of the first letters to identify objects.

4–4½ Year Skills

Learning

- Makes clear comparisons between two objects using one characteristic at a time, such as 'fatter' and 'thinner', 'heavier' and 'lighter'.
- Understands the difference between right and wrong but judges the morality of an action in terms of its consequences, not in terms of the intent.
- Offers his own solutions to everyday and hypothetical problems.
- Has an awareness of time, that the day is split into sequences which predictably follow each other and that certain events always occur at certain times of the day.
- Starts to show interest in the way that plants and animals grow, and asks you questions about life and death.

- Enjoys practical experiments involving weighing, measuring, mixing, dissolving and so on.

Social and Emotional

- Is more comfortable in the presence of familiar and unfamiliar adults, and can answer enquiries about himself appropriately.
- Has better communication skills, making good eye contact with the person speaking to him and replying in a clear voice.
- Boys tend to play with boys and girls with girls; gender stereotypes have formed – he has different expectations of the way boys and girls dress, behave and play.
- Friendships are more stable, and petty arguments during play with others are on the decline.
- Judges the merits of his own abilities by comparing himself to others he plays with; self-esteem is influenced by peer comparisons.

- Is able to take some responsibility for washing his hands and face regularly, brushing his teeth morning and night, and wearing fresh clothes (though you will need to check on these things).

Development
Movement

- Walks longer distances with you, especially if you make the journey more interesting by pointing out the sights.
- Engages in virtually all energetic play activities inlcuding climbing, sliding, balancing, throwing and catching.
- Skips from foot to foot and gives a hard kick to a large ball.
- Runs quickly upstairs – but don't let her do this in the opposite direction.
- Learns to use roller skates, but needs your support and encouragement until she is confident with them.
- Begins to master the difficult skill of using a skipping rope.
- May be able to ride a two-wheeled bicycle with stabilizers.

Hand–Eye Coordination

- Cuts more accurately with scissors, and can cut a large piece of paper into two pieces that are approximately the same size.
- Makes a good attempt at writing (not copying) her own first name, though the letters differ in size, the word goes up and down, and it's not very neat.
- Colouring-in is neater and closer to the border lines, with less of the colour outside the edge of the shape.
- Her drawings of people have much more detail than before; her picture of a house contains windows, a door and even a letter box.
- Uses a planned strategy to complete jigsaws instead of relying on luck to fit the pieces together.

- Once shown how, she can wash and dry her hands properly without supervision.
- Makes a good attempt at eating with a knife and fork.

Language

- Can use several thousand different words.
- Uses a broad range of words and sentences to convey her feelings to you; speech can become unclear if she is excited.
- Can give accurate biographical details to an adult who asks appropriate questions.
- In many ways, her speech and language

patterns resemble more closely those of an adult than those of a younger child.
- Cannot yet distinguish between a 'white lie' (told to protect another person's feelings) and an unacceptable lie (told to conceal the truth).
- Has clear views, expects you to listen carefully and to discuss things with her.

4½–5 Year Skills

Learning

- Realizes that when counting a row of objects, one number goes with one item, in sequence – she doesn't miss one out at this stage.
- May already be able to recognize and name written numbers up to five, and recite numbers up to ten.
- Improved concentration means she persists at an activity, without needing a break, until she is satisfied that it is finished.
- Enjoys learning the very basics of using a computer.
- Increased memory and stronger ability to organize herself allow her to plan ahead, perhaps to make preparations for an activity tomorrow.

- Sorts objects using two characteristics, such as colour and shape, at the same time.
- Is able to participate in board games involving a die – she can count the number of spots on the die and move the appropriate number of spaces on the board.

Social and Emotional

- Her natural instinct to be kind flourishes with your interest and approval, and she is more caring and sensitive towards others.
- Separates well from you when you drop her off at her childminder, nursery or playgroup.
- Values her friendships very much, and specifies particular children with whom she likes to play.
- Can cooperate with others to achieve an aim or complete a task.
- Is better able to deal with disagreements with other children assertively but not aggressively, if this is explained to her.
- Takes much more responsibility for herself, but still needs prompts and reminders from you.

Movement

The Development of Movement

Your pre-school child consolidates and advances the physical skills he developed in earlier years. Coordination challenges that eluded him before – such as hopping, skipping and balancing – are now accessible to him and he can attempt many of these activities. Of course he has a long way to go before he achieves total competence in these areas, but he is significantly more agile and athletic than before – the difference in movement ability between a toddler and a pre-school child is very noticeable. He loves practising these new physical skills, whether at home, at nursery or in the park.

Physical Transformation

The main reason for this maturation of movement skills is the underlying physical change that occurs between the ages of 2½ and 5 years. Your child becomes taller, with an accompanying increase in size – he probably grows around 8cm in height each year and puts on about 3kg in weight. His head size becomes smaller in proportion to the rest of his body, and his face broadens in preparation for the second set of teeth which will come through in a couple of years. Neurological changes take place in the brain, spine and nervous system as well.

The combined effect of all these normal physical changes is that your child becomes leaner and more agile. His body is in better shape and is stronger, with less fat to slow him down, and he can take part in energetic physical activity for longer without tiring. You'll also notice that during this period the size of his toddler's tummy decreases – this, too, adds to the increased agility of his arm and leg movements.

Many parents worry that their child doesn't eat enough to keep pace with this physical transformation. Such concerns are usually unnecessary. Your growing child almost certainly has an adequate daily intake of food and drink, but a routine check with your family doctor should allay any anxieties.

The Daredevil

Your child's improved physical skills mean that he wants to run and climb around every potential play area (and it doesn't matter whether it's an 'official' play area, such as his bedroom or a park, or an 'unofficial' play area, such as your kitchen or the other side of the street). At this age, he delights in using his improved motor skills, even when the activity is potentially hazardous.

Right: If your child is naturally adventurous, safe outdoor play equipment will provide the perfect opportunity for him to explore without endangering himself.

Many parents find that their child becomes a bit of a daredevil at this stage, as a result of typical pre-school enthusiasm.

Make sure he has plenty of opportunities to explore safely, so that he doesn't need to put himself at risk in order to achieve adventure and excitement. Well-structured outdoor play areas with swings and roundabouts, climbing frames and balancing logs are great fun and help to keep his curiosity stimulated – and the beauty is that they are designed with safety in mind.

Above: At 3 years and above, children are inclined to try out their physical skills anywhere, so be aware of danger areas.

Take him along to a leisure class, such as swimming, gymnastics or any other type of sport. Choose a well-supervised class that offers a safe, secure environment. Energy and enthusiasm are encouraged in these activities, not frowned upon. Although your child might be reluctant to go along at first, he'll soon settle in once he realizes the fun that awaits him.

Give your child lots of praise when you see him play energetically but safely – when you see him setting his own limits. Point out, for instance, how pleased you are that he only went half-way up the climbing frame because he wasn't sure how he would get down. Give him a cuddle when he remembers to walk along the street, instead of running wildly.

It is not easy to strike a balance between protecting your child so much that he becomes afraid to take part in energetic play, and letting him go until he reaches a point where he is at risk. A combination of sensible guidelines about keeping safe, coupled with positive directions about how to have adventures without danger, is the most effective strategy.

Timid

Some children are by nature timid and are afraid to explore wide open spaces in the park or adventure playground. You know the excitement that awaits your anxious child if he would only be bold enough to venture onto the climbing frame or kick the ball against the wall. But if your child is timid, he misses out on a wide range of stimulating activities.

Resist the temptation to push him too hard, too quickly. If he is genuinely afraid of hurting himself or of falling over, then he will freeze if pressurized to be more adventurous. Far better to use gentle, sensitive persuasion – sarcasm or ridicule about his timid behaviour will only make matters worse. He needs to feel that you are on his side, ready to guide him instead of laughing at him. Bear in mind that your timid child will be more willing to extend the limits of his physical skills when there is adult supervision. For example, he will be less afraid to learn to swim in a pool that has attendants and when you (or an instructor) are in the pool beside him.

Below: As your child gets more agile he will become more creative in his play, making playground equipment potentially hazardous even for a 5 year old.

Movement

Age	Skill
2½–3 years	Her increased leg and muscle strength means that she can jump more confidently into the air from a standing position and land without falling over.
	She can coordinate her arm, leg and whole-body movements so that she can carry out more than one physical task competently at the same time.
	Large outdoor apparatus excites her because it gives her a chance to demonstrate her increased physical skills to you while practising them at the same time.
3–3½ years	Her legs are stronger and she can coordinate her feet movements more effectively in order to propel a pedal toy slowly along the ground, as long as the surface is even.
	Her balance and coordination are more mature, giving her more confidence when it comes to jumping. She tries harder and achieves more.
	New movement skills emerge. Her face is a picture of total concentration as she carries out more complex activities that involve difficult balance.
3½–4 years	Her agility and coordination give her enough confidence to try out all the items in the outdoor play area, instead of restricting herself to just a few familiar toys.
	Manoeuvring herself on stairs is no longer such a challenge for your child. She steadily moves up and down them in a more mature, confident manner.

53

MOVEMENT

From 2½ to 5 Years

What to Do

Stand on a level, carpeted surface with your child facing you. Let her watch you jump high in the air, both feet pushing off the ground at the same time. Ask her to do this as well – the chances are that she can jump at least 8cm from the floor.

Give your child a toy wheelbarrow, one that she can hold firmly in both hands. Watch as she pushes this around the room, or perhaps in the garden. You'll see that she can walk forwards while steering the wheelbarrow around any obstacle in her way.

She'll take any opportunity she can to play on climbing frames, tunnels, ladders and slides, especially if you are watching, so provide plenty of time for this type of play. Don't be surprised, however, if she occasionally asks you for help when she suddenly realizes that she is unsure how to get back down again.

She will happily sit on a tricycle and turn the pedals with her feet, moving herself and the toy a few metres forward. You may need to remind her to keep the wheel pointing forwards, however, or she may inadvertently make the challenge harder for herself.

Walk with your child up to the second step of the flight of stairs in your house. Then turn around, so that you stand beside each other facing downwards. Having seen you jump two stairs at a time with both feet together, your child does this too.

Not only can she stand on her tiptoes for several seconds without putting her heels on the ground, she can also walk forward on her tiptoes if you break the action down into stages for her. Your child can probably take six or seven paces like this before stopping for a short break. Her balance is good.

She wants to climb onto the swing (although she needs you to push her gently back and forth), to go much nearer to the top of the climbing frame, and to run as fast as she can across the large, flat grassy areas in the park. Help and encourage her in these endeavours.

Encourage her to concentrate, so that she is able to walk upstairs and downstairs putting one foot on each step at a time. At first, she places her hand on the banister or wall for support all the time while moving on the stairs, but she gradually becomes steadier.

Movement

Age	Skill
	Ball games interest her more now. Her movement skills enable her to take part in ball-related activities that were previously too demanding.
4–4½ years	By now your child's balance, muscles, leg strength and limb coordination is sufficient for her to make a reasonable attempt at hopping along the ground. She can also walk along a narrow straight line.
	She makes an attempt at using a skipping rope, though this is very challenging because it involves such a combination of movement, balance and coordination skills.
	Your child can control her running movements so that she can maintain a good steady speed while still managing to swerve in order to avoid obstacles in her path.
4½–5 years	Her movement abilities mean that she can take part in virtually all energetic play activities, at least to some extent.
	Your child copes with basic tests of agility, due to her confidence, movement skills and general maturity.
	She is willing to try new games and toys involving movement, though she will need your support and encouragement as she learns how to use them.

From 2½ to 5 Years

What to Do

Give her a selection of balls – some small, some large, some soft, some harder. She likes to kick them along the ground or pick them up and throw them. Catching a ball is difficult: she tries to grab it to her chest using both arms, occasionally dropping it.

Show her how to position herself to stand on one foot while the other is raised off the ground and held slightly behind her. She can then hop perhaps three or four paces before putting both feet back on the ground. Also draw a straight chalk line for her to walk along.

Show her how to hold the ends of the rope in both hands, bring it from behind her over her head, and then jump over the rope as it nears her feet. She'll burst out laughing as the rope tangles around her feet. This skill needs lots of practice.

Ask her to run to you, from one side of the room to the other, without banging into any of the furniture. She can move quickly, turning to the left or right as necessary, without stopping or falling over – she is very pleased with herself.

She loves climbing to the top of the climbing frame, going up the ladder to the top of the slide and then sliding all the way down, trying to make the swing move back and forwards as she sits in it, and running all over the place at every opportunity. Provide safe access to large play apparatus in the garden or the park.

Apart from hopping several paces without over-balancing, she can skip from foot to foot, run quickly upstairs (though don't let her do this in the opposite direction) and give a hard kick to a large ball, making it move along the ground. Provide her with opportunities to explore all these activities.

Buy your child a solid pair of toy roller skates, and help her attach them firmly to her feet. At first she wants you to hold her hand and pull her along, but her confidence grows steadily and soon she is able to move herself very slowly without any help.

Stimulating Movement: 2½ to 3 Years

Your child's improved movement skills heighten his enthusiasm for energetic play. He is keen to run around with other children at every opportunity and shows both determination and daring on large play apparatus, such as a ladder and slide or a climbing frame. At times his ambition outstrips his ability – he may need your help if he gets stuck half-way.

TOO ENTHUSIASTIC

Some children are naturally more exuberant during energetic play than others; they like to push the other children, wrestle with them, and roll on the ground whenever they can. This is not intended as aggression, simply as play. However, a child on the receiving end of these acts of exuberance may become upset.

If you notice that your 3-year-old is very boisterous when playing with his pals, gently advise him that his friends may not like such rough play. Encourage him to think about their feelings and to watch whether or not they seem to be having fun. This increases his sensitivity towards them.

Suitable Suggestions

Aside from letting your child test out his improving movement skills during free play – and this is crucial to his physical development – you can also take a more hands-on approach by offering some direction. As a game, ask your child to copy your actions. For instance, you can wave your arms in the air, stand on one foot, bend down and touch your toes. Provide him with lots of physical actions to copy. Of course, some of these will be too difficult for him, but he'll have great fun trying to imitate you. Remember to keep these types of exercises a game, not a lesson; as long as you have a light-hearted approach, your child will be

Below: A home-made tunnel or house using chairs, tables and blankets makes a great piece of improvised play equipment for indoors.

happy to get involved. If he thinks his performance is under intense scrutiny, he'll quickly lose interest.

Use your garden, or the park, to its full extent. Even if there is no large play apparatus available, grassed areas can serve as a mini sports ground for your enthusiastic and energetic 3-year-old. Encourage him to run from one spot to the next as fast as he can. Although he is relatively slow and wobbly as he moves, your delight in his performance makes him feel like a top athlete. Children this age often love running round in medium-sized circles when there is an adult in the centre. Call out encouraging comments as he runs round. Make sure he

Above: As this 3-year-old boy copies the actions made by his 5-year-old sister it is clear that his movements are not yet as precise as hers.

rests every so often, before going on to the next activity.

His arm and leg movements also benefit from practice at ball games. For instance, when your child stands still, place a large ball just in front of his dominant foot (the one he kicks with) and ask him to kick it as hard as he can. He should be able to maintain his balance while doing so, but don't be surprised if he topples over. As he improves his kicking ability, place the ball further away from him so that he has to move towards it before striking it. Each time, extend the distance between your child and the ball.

❖❖❖❖❖❖❖ Top·Tips ❖❖❖❖❖❖❖

1. Keep him calm. Your child may experience frustration if he can't master a physical play activity. When you see him angry or tearful, calm him, remove him from that activity and let him return to it later when he is more settled.

2. Join in with his play at times. It doesn't matter if your own coordination skills are limited – they will certainly be good enough to stimulate your 3-year-old's interest. Play ball games with him, or trot beside him as he runs.

3. Indulge his favourites. Your child probably has particular energetic activities that he enjoys playing over and over again. That's fine (assuming you are happy with the activity) because each play episode increases his existing movement skills.

4. Encourage play with others. Whether at home with his pals or at nursery or playgroup with others his own age, experience of playing energetically with his peers is one of the best ways to stimulate and advance your child's coordination.

5. Make him think about safety. Your child's more mature level of physical skills potentially places him at higher risk when playing. Each time he plays outdoors, gently – but firmly – remind him to take care of himself and to remain safe.

Q&A

Q My child is 2½ years old. Should he be able to hop?

A Most children do not develop the ability to hop until they are between the ages of 3 and 4 years, though there is no harm in preparing your child's readiness for this skill. For instance, at the age of 2½ years you could ask him to try balancing with one foot raised off the ground.

Q Compared to my friend's child, my child seems to be fatter and slower. When will he start to thin out?

A He is already in the process of losing his 'puppy fat' – this happens as part of natural growth during this period. What matters at this stage is not so much his body size but his attitude. If he is enthusiastic, you have no need to worry.

🧸🚒 **Toys:** pedal toys, soft football, climbing frame, bat and ball, garden toys, soft play-mat for rolling on

Think about your own attitudes to this. If you consider that boys are naturally more aggressive during physical play – and vice versa for girls – then your own child may conform to this expectation.

Stimulating Movement: 3 to 3½ Years

Your child's movement skills become more sophisticated and controlled and her learning ability also increases. She combines these two areas of development so that she can take part in a varied range of activities. Instead of trying to acquire a new physical skill come what may, she is more able to listen to your advice and to plan a strategy for reaching her goal.

Suitable Suggestions

At this age, you should try to establish the idea in your child's mind that exercise is part of her daily routine. She doesn't need to go in the car from place to place, or be driven up to the front door of the nursery each session. Walking every day should be normal practice. If she gets used to taking part in physical movement at the age of 3, she is less likely to become a couch potato later on.

Use music to make movement activities more fun. For instance, dance along with your child to her favourite music. Her lack of inhibition means that she willingly twists and turns her body and shakes her arms and legs in time to the beat; she's not at all bothered

Below: Dancing is a wonderful way to encourage children to use their bodies in different ways, perhaps pretending to be an animal or a plane.

about what others might think of her. Every so often, ask her to copy a particular dance movement that you make. This is simply another form of energetic play that stimulates her arm, leg and body movements.

Be prepared to teach new movement skills if she struggles to learn them spontaneously. Take walking on tiptoes, for instance. Your child's initial reaction to this challenge might be to rush at it, the end result being that she falls over and loses her confidence. Break the activity down into small stages. First, she should stand steady with both feet firmly on the ground and then raise her heels slightly. Once she is comfortable she can raise them higher, and so on, each time getting closer and closer to standing on her tiptoes.

Eventually she will be confident about standing independently on her tiptoes.

The next stage is to teach her how to walk in that position. Encourage her to move one foot forward a few centimetres only, while the other is stationary. Then the forward step can become longer, and then she can start to move her back foot a few centimetres. In other words, gradually lead her towards mastering the movement skill. Be patient with your child. You'll find that she learns at her own natural pace.

Below: By 3½ most children have sufficient strength and coordination to kick a ball quite forcefully and some can even master this while they or the ball are on the move.

Q & A

Q My child is 3½ years old and she insists on climbing all over the furniture. What should I do?

A Make it clear that climbing over the furniture is not acceptable. Point out to her the risk of possible injury to herself and the damage she could do to the furniture. At the same time, suggest a play area in which she can exercise her climbing skills freely.

Q Should I expect a growth spurt in my child at this age?

A No. A growth spurt – a rapid period of growth in your child's height, weight and body volume – occurs at two points during childhood. The first takes place approximately between birth and 2 years, and the second during adolescence. Her growth rate is steady between the ages of 2½ and 5.

Toys: tricycle, other pedal toys, plastic bowling pins and ball, balls, toy cars, plastic playhouse

⋄⋄⋄⋄⋄⋄⋄ Top·Tips ⋄⋄⋄⋄⋄⋄⋄

1. Encourage planning. If your child faces an activity or challenge involving movement, suggest that she thinks what to do instead of rushing headlong into it. A few seconds' planning could be all that is needed in order to ensure success.

2. Play on a see-saw with her. Moving gently up and down on a see-saw uses her leg muscles (as she pushes off), her arm muscles (as she holds on) and builds her confidence. Keep the movements steady and even.

3. Roll a ball towards her. Face your child, with 3–4m between you, and softly roll a football towards her. Ask her to kick the ball as it reaches her, without stopping it first – she may manage this with some practice.

4. Let her seat herself. She is now capable of climbing into her own chair at mealtimes and twisting her body until she achieves a comfortable position for eating. Resist the temptation to place her in the chair yourself.

5. Walk on slopes. Make sure that you and your child don't only walk on perfectly flat areas. Strolling up a slight incline strengthens her leg muscles and builds up her stamina for movement. She copes with a small slope.

Stimulating Movement: 3½ to 4 Years

Your child is much more confident with activities involving movement skills. He knows that his balance, coordination and muscle strength is greater and he eagerly takes part in kicking, throwing and catching games. This same enthusiasm is extended to outdoor play, where he becomes more adventurous with the play equipment. Stairs are no longer a major hurdle for your 4-year-old.

THE OTHERS ARE BETTER

Once your child attends playgroup or nursery, it's only natural that he compares himself to others – and that includes comparing his movement skills. His self-esteem may dip if he realizes that some of his peers are more agile and athletic than him. Reassure him in these circumstances.

Encourage him to continue to join in to the best of his ability. Explain that he will get better with practice and that he's great even though a couple of the others can do things he can't. He will gradually learn to accept that individual differences exist, and that he has his own level of skills.

Suitable Suggestions

Your child wants to use the whole range of movement skills in his repertoire, but probably needs suggestions from you. Show him the wide variety of energetic play activities now available to him, as he may not think of them himself.

For instance, he can hop alongside you, though don't jump too high or he may fall over as he tries to imitate you. Your child finds hopping easier when wearing outdoor shoes because the soles provide a more stable landing area. However, he should also hop on a carpeted surface without wearing socks or shoes as this involves more of his foot muscles. You could also place a small object on the floor and invite him to walk up to it quickly, then pick it up and hand it to you.

Ask your child to fetch you an item from upstairs, and remind him to concentrate as he brings it to you. Just to be on the safe side, stand at the bottom of the stairs as he is about to descend with the object in his hand. Tell him to use either the banister or the wall as support while moving downwards, and add that he should move slowly. This is a challenging task for your 4-year-old because both parts of your request – the carrying and the descending – require his full attention. But he will achieve it as long as he takes his time and concentrates all the way through.

Left: Hopping requires a good sense of balance and by 3½ your child may be ready to try this, although some children may still find it beyond them at first.

Left: Take advantage of any opportunity to improve your child's movement skills. Running alongside you will give her the confidence to run faster.

If possible, arrange for him to play on a 'bouncy castle' at a play centre. This air-inflated piece of apparatus allows him to practise jumping and falling without any risk of injury to himself. Encourage him to watch out for others, though. You'll notice that although he may be timid to start with, he becomes much more energetic with his jumps as his confidence builds. This will improve his jumping ability when he is on the ground. Likewise, try to get him access to a trampoline. A child this age loves jumping up and down on it – he can also bounce up and down while on his knees.

Below: Learning to swim at an early age has many benefits for a child – as well as being confident in the water she is safer, too.

✧✧✧✧✧✧ Top ✧ Tips ✧✧✧✧✧✧

1. Play throwing and catching. Stand a metre or so away from your child, facing him. Gently throw a medium-sized soft ball to him. He may be able to catch it with both hands – once he has the ball in his hands, he should throw it towards you.

2. Run in time to music. Pick a song that he likes (one with a steady beat) and suggest that he runs beside you as you keep up with the beat. Sing as you run. He'll keep going until he is breathless.

3. Establish good nutrition. Your child likes to eat lots of snacks, especially after energetic play. Provide him with milk and fruit juice instead of fizzy drinks to quench his thirst. Encourage him to avoid sweets and foods with additives.

4. Build a small obstacle course. In good weather, use the garden whenever possible. Construct an obstacle course with objects for him to run around, climb over and duck under. Time him as he progresses through it.

5. Enrol him in a swimming class. Your child may have already learned to swim, but whether he has or not, he'll benefit from instruction by a qualified swimming trainer. His confidence in the water grows steadily.

Q&A

Q I've heard that children who grow faster are smarter. Is that true?

A Some studies have found that children who have very quick growth patterns in early childhood do tend to score slightly higher in school tests than children with a slower growth rate. Yet there are plenty of small children who are brighter than their larger peers. Growth rate is only one small factor.

Q Why is it that when my 4-year-old tries to throw the ball to me it ends up going behind him?

A When he throws a ball, he has to decide on the moment of release from his hand. Like many others this age, he is so intent on getting force behind his throw that he mistimes the release – hence the ball goes in the wrong direction.

Toys: climbing frame, plastic stepping stones, toy digging tools, play tunnel to crawl through, ride-on toy

Stimulating Movement: 4 to 4½ Years

Your child is on the go all the time – no matter how much she runs around, she never tires. And she doesn't need any more sleep. You'll probably find that your child spends more time in energetic movement play than she does on games that involve her sitting still. The feeling of achievement she gets from using her movement skills adds to her enjoyment.

Suitable Suggestions

Now is a good time to begin playing bat-and-ball games with your child. Buy her a large bat or racket and a very soft ball. When she turns the racket flat and horizontal with the ground, place the ball on top so that when she moves the racket up in the air the ball flies from it. Do the same again, only this time drop the ball onto the racket from a few centimetres above it. Then throw the ball, underarm style, onto the racket from about a metre away, while encouraging your child to

Below: Once your child has got the hang of hitting a ball with a bat, a whole new range of play opportunities open up for him.

swipe at it. This is a complex task, which she probably finds difficult.

Think about gentle jogging together in the park. She'll thoroughly enjoy this activity with you, and will be able to keep up if your pace is slow enough for her little legs. Tell her how pleased you are to be running with her. Or just go for a brisk walk together. Take her to the local swimming baths if she enjoys that activity.

At infant school, she'll play team games. Introduce her to these now. Organize two teams (even if there are only two members in each) and set up a simple challenge, such as to run up to a chair, clutch one of the plastic blocks sitting on it and return to the team so that the next person can do this. Team games

Above: Team games are simple to organize and great fun – as well as stimulating physical activity they also encourage a sense of cooperation.

make winning or losing dependent on the overall performance of all the members. She'll try her hardest to do well. Comfort her if she gets upset because her team didn't win.

During free play with her friends, she'll spontaneously play at football, climbing, running, crawling, rolling or skipping. She enjoys playing in the playground of the local park at every opportunity, though she has plenty of this type of play in nursery. If you are at all concerned that she doesn't get enough exercise, take her out yourself at weekends.

Below: At this age, your child's movement and coordination skills have reached quite an advanced level and she is able to manoeuvre a swing by herself.

Top · Tips

1. **Make a hurdle to jump over.** Tie a piece of elastic between two chairs, a few centimetres from the ground. Once she has successfully jumped over that, increase the height of the elastic each time. If she hits the elastic, it will simply stretch.

2. **Ask your child to push the supermarket trolley, under your supervision.** Pick one that has smooth-running wheels. Position your child so that she grips the handle firmly with both hands, then invite her to push. Help her steer it accurately.

3. **Let her propel the swing herself.** This isn't easy, but she might manage. Explain to her that she should keep her body still as she bends it slightly forwards and then backwards. With a bit of luck, the swing will gently gather momentum.

4. **Play movement games.** Make up games that involve her hopping, running, skipping and walking. You can even do this in time to music. The main thing is that she has fun using her movement skills.

5. **Praise her for success and effort.** When you see her try hard at a physical activity – whether she is successful or not – give her a big hug so that she knows you are delighted with her.

Q & A

Q Is it better to concentrate on one movement skill at a time or to encourage lots of different ones simultaneously?

A Too much focus on one skill can put your child under unnecessary pressure. And anyway, she'll learn a new skill best when she practises it for a few minutes, has a long break and then practises again. Those rest periods in between have a positive effect.

Q My child trips a lot when she runs. Could there be a problem?

A The reason she falls is more likely to be lack of concentration than any difficulty with balance and coordination. She's so busy looking excitedly at everything around her that she doesn't keep an eye on minor obstacles. Encourage her to scan below eye level as well when she runs.

Toys: bat and ball, skipping rope, small plastic hoops to throw and catch, football, plastic roller skates

Stimulating Movement: 4½ to 5 Years

Your child is ready to take part in all the physical activities of the infant school. His movement skills are sufficient for him to walk around the school building comfortably, negotiate any flights of stairs, walk while carrying objects (for instance, in the classroom or in the dining room) and enjoy the wide open spaces of the infant playground.

ACTIVITY AND REST

As your child approaches – and then reaches – school age, he spends more time sitting down than ever before. Concentration is an important factor influencing progress, and he needs to learn to sit calmly while giving his full attention to the activity in front of him.

But he still needs time to run around energetically. Of course you will do your best to get him into a good frame of mind for school and to prepare him for listening intently to the teacher's instructions. Make sure, however, you build time into his daily routine for periods of high activity, too.

Suitable Suggestions

This is a good time to sharpen your child's existing movement skills. Give him plenty of opportunities to practise basic skills such as throwing and catching, kicking a ball, running, walking and any other physical activity he enjoys, such as swimming, gymnastics or dancing. Do this at home, out in the street or in the local park. If there are any movement skills that are not as strong as you would like them to be, give a few minutes' extra attention to them each day.

Below: As she gets older your child will be able to use a much wider variety of play equipment and will be spurred on by watching other children.

Playing with other children is very important either at home, at nursery or in a supervised activity class. As well as learning from social interactions, your child is also able to measure his own level of physical agility against his peers, and this provides him with reassurance.

Try to improve a couple of his more sophisticated movement skills, such as using a skipping rope or moving himself on roller skates. He'll have played with these pieces of equipment before, but as he approaches his fifth birthday he should be able to develop a better mastery of them. Don't let him give up just because the rope keeps catching on his

Left: At 5 these girls are able to use roller skates. Your child will still need your help when attempting something like this for the first time.

feet or because the roller skates seem to stick in every small crevice in the ground. Gently persuade him to persist until he notices the improvement himself. He'll have to acquire new movement skills during physical education lessons in school, and working at these challenges now teaches him a strategy for learning more complicated physical tasks later on.

Don't forget static activities involving arm, leg and body movements, because these also enhance your child's sense of self and help him to understand both the limits and potential of his own physical development. Ask your child to stand upright with his arms by his sides and then touch his toes with the tips of his fingers, without bending his knees as he does so. He might over-balance at first, or perhaps try to bend his knees. Other examples of useful static exercises include balancing on one leg – and then while in that position, swaying gently in a circle.

Below: At this age children are more likely to persevere with a toy like a skipping rope, trying the actions repeatedly until they master it.

✦✦✦✦✦✦✦ Top·Tips ✦✦✦✦✦✦✦

1. Keep it fun. Although you need to prepare your child physically for starting school, these activities and exercises should be fun. He could become anxious if he thinks the expectations at school will be too great for him to meet.

2. Walk longer distances. This is a good way to build up his physical stamina. Instead of the usual amount of time you and your child spend walking together, gradually add on an extra couple of minutes before you turn round for the return journey.

3. Teach movement skills in small steps. New movement skills don't appear from nowhere – they develop gradually over time. So don't expect your child suddenly to be able to do something he couldn't do before. Show him step by step.

4. Combine balance and movement. Give him more demanding movement challenges. For instance, draw a thick, zigzag chalk line on the ground and ask him to walk along this while carrying a nearly full glass of water.

5. Consider a two-wheeler. Your child may be willing to try pedalling a two-wheeled bicycle, assuming it has smaller stabilizing wheels attached to it. Stand right beside him as he starts to push with his feet just in case the bike topples over.

Hand–Eye

Coordination

The Importance of Hand–Eye Coordination

As your growing child progresses through the pre-school years, hand control becomes increasingly important, not just because it helps her become more independent (for instance, she can undo large buttons without asking for your help) but also because it is linked to problem-solving (she can manipulate jigsaw pieces in order to complete the puzzle) and to learning (her ability to hold a pencil correctly and to draw patterns on paper gradually transforms into basic writing skills).

Maturation

Don't forget that your child's progress with hand–eye coordination depends on the interaction between the stimulation and encouragement she receives daily, her physical and neurological development, and her motivation. These three different dimensions need to be carefully balanced before she can move from one stage to the next.

In particular, she will not be able to write like a 5-year-old when she is only 3 years old, no matter how hard she tries, because she simply does not have the muscular and neurological maturity to make such fine hand movements. If you put your child under pressure, for example,

Right: Even in general play you will notice improvements in hand–eye coordination.

to 'write neatly like your big sister', you run the risk of turning off her interest in writing altogether. Instead of setting a target that is based on an older child's drawing and writing achievements, look carefully at your child's ability and then encourage her to develop it a little bit further.

Paints or Crayons?

You may also find that she prefers using paints to crayons, and so doesn't draw fine lines the way you'd like her to. Paint brushes are often more interesting than pencils or crayons to a child, for a number of reasons. First, it's easier to make a large, colourful picture with sweeping brush strokes than it is with a crayon – pictures are created more quickly with paints. Second, a chunky paint brush is easier to grip and doesn't require

such fine finger control. And third, painting has a wonderful messy side to it that pre-school children generally adore.

Your child needs experience of painting as well as drawing and writing; each activity develops skills that help the other, so let her choose between a selection of paints, crayons and pencils. As long as she dabbles in each of these, her hand–eye coordination will progress at a satisfactory rate.

Left or Right?

Your child's hand preference – that is, whether she prefers to use her left hand or her right hand – will probably be fully established by the time she starts school (though approximately 10 per cent of children who start the infant class still switch between their left and their right hand).

Although psychologists don't know for sure whether handedness is inborn or learned, there is some evidence that it is linked to the two

Above: Nearly all children love finger painting – even those who do not show much interest in drawing or colouring.

halves of the brain. For instance, in right-handed children, the left side of the brain may have a stronger relationship with the entire right side of the body. Whatever the true explanation, however, you'll already have noticed her established hand preference from around the age of 2 years onwards, perhaps even before then. Resist any urge you

Below: Although being right-handed is the norm, you should never discourage your child from using her left hand if that comes more naturally to her.

may feel to transform your 'leftie' into a 'rightie' before she starts school. That would be a mistake.

True, we live in a right-handed world. True, learning to write is more challenging for a left-handed child because she tends to drag her hand over her writing or drawing, often smudging it. Yet there is some evidence that forcing your left-handed child to use her right hand – either when she is with you at home or at nursery – could create speech problems. And aside from that, battling with her to go against her natural preference will damage your relationship and will make her feel there is something wrong with her. All in all, it's best to leave the matter of hand preference entirely to your child.

Comparison

Now that your child mixes more with other children – whether it's friends who come over to her house to play or joining in with others at nursery – she compares herself to her peers. She judges the worth of her own paintings and drawings by the extent to which they measure up against those of the other children with whom she plays. This can have a positive or negative effect – positive if she considers her creative efforts to be at least as good as the

others', negative if she believes that her own drawing ability is inferior to her friends' creative talents.

A 4-year-old's enthusiasm for challenges involving hand–eye coordination will rapidly evaporate in the face of apparently better efforts by her pal standing next to her. And when she loses belief in her own abilities, she'll be very reluctant to paint, draw or write the next time an opportunity arises.

That's why she needs bags of encouragement from you to continue with activities involving hand control, whether it's threading small wooden beads onto a lace, cutting paper into small pieces with scissors, copying her name onto a piece of paper, colouring in a shape or line drawing, or completing dot-to-dot puzzles. Your positive comments boost her motivation.

Improvements in hand–eye coordination typically occur steadily but slowly between the ages of 3 and 5 years, making them difficult to detect. Your child might need you to point out that she is now much more adept at cutting her food with a knife than she was, say, a couple of months ago. She needs you to draw her attention to these small steps forward.

Hand–Eye Coordination

Age	Skill

2½–3 years

Your child likes cutting up pieces of paper with scissors, but he has great difficulty holding the scissors and also moving them in an effective cutting motion.

Even at this age, his hand control has improved to the point where his drawings are often recognizable – you can probably work out what he has tried to draw.

Your child likes to help you around the house, sometimes simply copying whatever you do and sometimes actually carrying out a practical task for you.

3–3½ years

When he concentrates hard, he holds small objects with a steady hand and moves them quite precisely without dropping them from his grasp.

Scissors are more manageable for him now, partly due to the increased size of his fingers and hands but also because his grip is more mature.

Button fastening and unfastening is no longer such a mystery to your child. He wants to do things like this by himself and he is willing to try hard at such tasks.

3½–4 years

His drawing skills have advanced so much that he accurately copies many of the basic lines that are part of written letters, even though he can't form complete letters.

His increased hand–eye coordination enables him to use a piece of cutlery in each hand, to eat in a tidier way and to drink from a cup without any spillage at all.

From 2½ to 5 Years

What to Do

Buy him a pair of child-safe scissors, the type with large, moulded handles suitable for his small fingers and with protective covers on the edges of the blades to minimize injury. He needs lots of practice before he is able to grip the handles properly.

Give him specific patterns or shapes to copy. Let him see you draw a plain circle on a piece of paper, and then ask him to do the same. His drawing will definitely be of a circle, but don't expect it to be perfectly round. The ends may not join up.

Use his interest in housework to consolidate his hand–eye coordination. His hand control is good enough for him to dust a tabletop or any smooth surface, to put toys back into the toy box, and even to put cutlery on the table for your lunchtime meal.

Place a small pile of wooden blocks in front of him and ask him to build them up, one on top of the other. He probably balances eight or nine blocks this way before his mini-tower eventually topples over. He enjoys practising this until he gets it right.

Give him a pair of child-sized scissors and let him place them on his fingers himself. Once he tells you that he is holding them comfortably, give him a large piece of thick paper to cut. He is now able to make the blades cut through the paper.

Fasten the large buttons on a shirt or cardigan (the larger, the better), hand it to him closed and suggest that he tries to undo the buttons. At first, he simply pulls them apart. After a couple of attempts, however, he begins to use his fingers to open them.

Give your child lots of pencil practice with copying circles, vertical straight lines, horizontal straight lines and continuous undulating lines. Show him how these can be put together in many different ways in order to make varied attractive patterns.

Make a point of insisting that he uses cutlery at mealtimes, despite his desire to finger feed. By now he probably holds a spoon in one hand, a fork in the other, and combines them both to bring food from his plate directly to his mouth.

Hand–Eye Coordination

Skill

He loves challenging activities that involve hand–eye coordination and is prepared to try them several times in order to achieve success.

Your child's advanced understanding coupled with his better hand control means that he wants to write his name as long as he has a written example he can copy.

He is full of his own importance, determined to cope with basic self-help tasks without your help. Your child prefers to wash, dress and feed himself independently.

He manipulates modelling clay into many different shapes, using his fingers to mould it instead of simply shaping it with pressure from his hands.

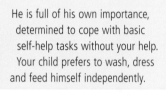

Your child has acquired many of the early writing skills required for managing the curriculum of the infant class, and he continues to improve with each passing month.

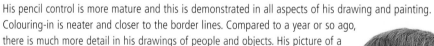

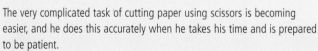

His pencil control is more mature and this is demonstrated in all aspects of his drawing and painting. Colouring-in is neater and closer to the border lines. Compared to a year or so ago, there is much more detail in his drawings of people and objects. His picture of a house contains windows, a door and even a letter box; his drawing of a person has a nose, eyes, ears, hair, feet, hands and even fingers.

The very complicated task of cutting paper using scissors is becoming easier, and he does this accurately when he takes his time and is prepared to be patient.

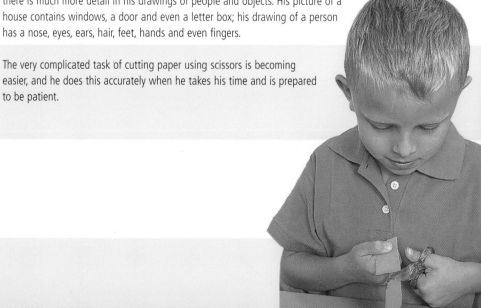

From 2½ to 5 Years

What to Do

Give your child a bundle of coloured wooden beads that have a hole drilled through them. Ask your child to make you a necklace by threading several of them onto a lace. This isn't easy, especially when the threaded beads pull heavily against the lace.

Let him see you write his name very neatly in large, clear lettering at the top of a plain white piece of paper. Invite him to write the same underneath. His letter formation is untidy and off the horizontal, but there is no doubt that it is his name.

Encourage him to be independent in terms of personal hygiene and household tasks. At this age, he may be able to wash his hands and face before bedtime, to put cutlery on the table and clear up dishes after a meal, and to lift very small items from the floor when tidying up.

When you offer ideas for objects to make from modelling clay, encourage him to add details, such as a nose on a face, hair on a head or shoes on the feet. He creates these small items from the clay and then neatly attaches them to the appropriate place.

As they approach their fifth birthday, many children are able to make a recognizable attempt at writing their own first name without copying – the letters differ in size, the word goes up and down, it's not terribly neat, but he is proud to put his name down on paper. Encourage him in this endeavour.

Provide him with the materials – paints, chalks, crayons and pencils, plus plain and coloured paper and a large, flat surface – and plenty of opportunities to practise these skills.

Hand him a piece of paper and ask him to cut it into two pieces that are roughly the same size. When he completes this, take the larger section and ask him to do the same again. Repeat this until he tells you that the paper is too small to cut any more.

Stimulating Hand–Eye Coordination: 2½ to 3 Years

Your child knows her hand control has improved and she is prepared to do much more for herself as a result. She proudly shows you how she is able to hold a cup on her own, how she can pick things up from the floor using her thumb and index finger, and how she can try to dress and undress herself.

Different Toys

One of the helpful aspects of an inset board is that the outer frame guides your child towards the correct solution. Jigsaws are more challenging because the pieces can be combined in a whole variety of ways. The change from inset boards to jigsaws, therefore, requires new skills.

Start off with a very basic jigsaw, one that has chunky wooden pieces, an engaging picture and only two or three parts at most. Explain to your child that she should use the picture to decide which way the pieces join together. Once she has mastered these easier puzzles, gradually increase the number of pieces.

Suitable Suggestions

Do what you can to encourage your child to use her hand–eye coordination so that she becomes more independent. Personal hygiene is an area worth considering. The sorts of tasks involving hand control that she can begin to try for herself include undressing and dressing herself in the toilet (although don't be surprised to find her skirt is accidentally tucked into her pants) and

Left: Encourage your child to put on his own shoes – this is an everyday way for him to practise using his hands.

Below: Gluing pieces of paper is an activity children find engrossing and it helps them learn to manipulate small items.

washing and drying her hands (although she might splash more water than you expected).

Older children often need help in these areas and therefore your child may not be able to complete these self-help tasks without your support. She might like you to watch her, say, wash her hands so that you can guide her through it. Point out the different stages to her (for instance, first she must turn the tap on, then she must put both hands under the running water, then she should rub them together, and so on) and urge her to concentrate along the way.

Make sure she has lots of art and craft materials when playing. She probably reaches

Above: Children love to help you with 'real' household chores and they will watch and copy the way you do things.

for them without any prompting from you, but give her a bit of extra encouragement anyway. There is no doubt that her drawings have improved. For instance, she starts to put in some small details such as arms and legs on the human figures she sketches. Avoid mentioning to her that she has missed out the eyes, or the nose, or whatever – as far as she is concerned, the drawing is fine and she doesn't have the understanding needed to put in these other features. Resist any urges you have to instruct her on how to draw – she'll steadily get better as long as she has bags of opportunity for free drawing, painting and colouring-in.

Another useful activity for encouraging her hand control is crumpling, tearing and gluing. She never tires of tearing up pieces of paper, or crumpling little bits of coloured tissue paper and then gluing them onto a larger sheet of paper. Her little fingers work away eagerly at this. Display her creations in your house if possible.

Top Tips

1. Focus on colouring. Now that she's almost 3 years old, she should pay more attention to the accuracy of her crayon strokes and these should be closer to the outline of the shape. Suggest she watches the paper as she colours it in.

2. Think ahead. The reality is that although she is able to do more for herself, each action involving hand control takes time – and this may not be convenient if you are in a hurry. Try to plan ahead so that you are not rushed.

3. Give her household chores. There's no reason why your child should not hold a cloth to wipe a small tabletop or pick up the small toys that have been scattered across the floor as she played. She wants to help around the house.

4. Keep her calm. The more complex the task involving hand–eye coordination, the more effort, concentration and time is required. She may need your reassurance when she doesn't complete the activities as fast as she would like.

5. Think about enrolling at nursery. Nurseries accept children from the age of 3 years onwards (and many now admit them even earlier). Investigate this several months ahead because spaces are often limited.

Q & A

Q Should I be worried because my 3-year-old seems to struggle when trying to stack bricks?

A She will improve with practice. And remember that if her hands are sweating, or if she is a bit nervous, or even if the surface of the table is slippery, then stacking bricks becomes even more difficult.

Q Our child is aged 33 months but she still expects me to feed her, even though I know her hand control is good enough to feed herself. What should I do?

A The next time you place finger food in front of her, let her get on with it herself. If she looks to you for help, tell her she has to lift the food herself. Don't give in – and when she does put the food in her mouth, shower her with praise.

Toys: doll's tea set, farm animal and people play figures, pencils, crayons, paints and paper

Stimulating Hand–Eye Coordination: 3 to 3½ Years

The wide range of toys and games available to your child now that he has started attending nursery stimulates his hand control even further. He wants to try everything he sees, even though many of the items there are too challenging for him. His desire to keep up with the other children he plays with is a further incentive to improve his hand–eye coordination.

TEACHING PATIENCE

In the same way that you feel frustrated when that annoying piece of thread refuses to pass through the eye of the needle, your 3-year-old experiences inner tension when a hand-control challenge proves too difficult. Tears and temper may ensue when the small objects won't go where he wants.

Calm your child at these moments, reassure him that he has the ability to complete the task if he remains calm, and then encourage him to start again slowly. You could also suggest he leaves that particular activity for a few moments in order to compose himself – allow him to return to it later.

Suitable Suggestions

Your child's innate drive to become independent strengthens as he realizes that there are more things he can do by himself. You can help him by giving him small tasks that combine personal responsibility and hand control. When he tidies his toys encourage him to put them away neatly. Show him how to hold his toothbrush so that he can clean his teeth properly. Of course he still has a long way to go, but he will try hard to achieve targets you set for him.

At this age, his concentration has improved and he can persist at an activity for more

Below: Clapping games and action songs all help to improve a child's repertoire of hand movements.

than just a few minutes. This makes him ready for more challenging activities. Devise your own games for this purpose; for instance, put a pile of very small, round wooden beads on a saucer and ask him to move them one at a time onto another saucer close by. Watch his face screw up with intense concentration as he slowly tries to complete the task.

If he does manage to move the beads from one saucer to the other, you could repeat the

Left: When she is 3 or so you can encourage your child to brush her teeth more accurately, targeting top and bottom and back and front teeth.

Q My child's hand strength doesn't seem to be very good. How can I improve it?

A The power in his muscles will increase spontaneously as he matures, so you don't need to do anything special at all at the moment. However, you could play a game in which he grips a small soft ball in his hand and then squeezes it repeatedly. You can also encourage him to play with construction toys.

Q Is my son too old for finger painting now that he can hold a brush?

A Finger painting uses different parts of his hands and fingers compared to painting with a brush, so he should have an opportunity to take part in both activities (as long as you are prepared for the mess). It's also great fun, no matter how old he is.

Toys: jigsaws with more pieces, colouring-in books, small wooden beads, play figures and furniture

---

Above: At this age your child may have the patience and skill to move on to more complex puzzles with more and smaller pieces.

✦✦✦✦✦✦✦ Top·Tips ✦✦✦✦✦✦✦

1. Reassure him. He may be upset to discover he has made a mess of something even though he tried to be neat. Tell him you are pleased with his effort, and that he'll make less of a mess the next time.

2. Play finger games. Make up games involving finger and hand movements. For instance, his hands could be two spiders crawling their way along the table. He can clap his hands to copy you, each time making a different sound.

3. Roll modelling clay. His hand–eye coordination benefits from practice making clay shapes, or rolling lumps of clay with a small rolling pin. Once they are made, he can mash them up and start over again.

4. Ask him to bring items to you. He loves helping you, so use this to boost his hand control. For instance, he can unscrew a jar to bring you a biscuit or open a box to bring you a button.

5. Stack bricks in different patterns. Provide construction examples for him to copy, such as a number of bricks in the shape of a small train with a funnel, or in the shape of an house. He tries to imitate your design.

challenge, but on this occasion time him using a watch. Maybe he can do it a little faster the next time. It's important, however, to keep this play session fun, otherwise what should be a pleasant game could turn into an episode of frustration and anger. Let him know how delighted you are with his attempts at this activity. Make sure he doesn't take it all too seriously.

Jigsaws remain an effective way of improving hand control. Speak to the playgroup leaders or nursery staff to find out the level of jigsaw he plays with there. You may find that the ones he has at home are now too easy for him and that he requires puzzles with a greater number of pieces. If so, quietly remove the smaller jigsaws from his toy box and replace them with more advanced ones. He'll be delighted with any new puzzles you give him, especially if the picture grabs his interest.

Stimulating Hand–Eye Coordination: 3½ to 4 Years

The most remarkable change in your child's hand–eye coordination during this six-month period is her increased expectations of her own ability and performance. For instance, she plays more intricately with small doll's house furniture because she knows she can move the very small pieces more accurately, and she spends more time on her drawings because she delights in adding finer details.

DOT-TO-DOT

Joining dots together provides terrific practice in hand control, but most dot-to-dot books rely on a child's ability to recognize numbers and to know the number sequence. This means they are probably unsuitable for your child at 3½ years old, so make up your own patterns for her to complete.

Draw shapes such as a circle, square or triangle. Instead of drawing full lines, put a dot for each corner and several dots in between to give a rough outline. Explain to your child that she should join all the dots together in order to reveal the shape. If she is uncertain, show her what to do at first.

Suitable Suggestions

Achievement with hand control is more likely when your child has a good sitting position. Many of the activities she now enjoys using hand–eye coordination need her to be in a chair, to adopt a stable position and to lean over the toy or game so that she achieves maximum vision. But your child is used to rushing through things quickly, moving from one activity to another without organizing herself appropriately. You can help her achieve more success with her hand–eye

Below: This girl is able to play successfully with her toy drill but the expression on her face shows that she is having to concentrate hard on her hand movements.

Below: Give your 4-year-old plenty of different drawing materials. Sand can be used to practise writing or drawing skills and is also great fun.

coordination skills by encouraging her to sit properly and comfortably in a suitably sized chair while completing the task.

Explain to her that, for instance, moving small items of furniture from one room to another in her doll's house is easier when she sits in a chair facing it. Naturally she prefers to play this game standing up because she feels less constrained, but direct her towards a seated position anyway. She needs you to point this out to her at this stage. The same applies when she is drawing or colouring-in: suggest that she works at a table or desk, with her chair pulled close to it so that she is right over the toys she plays with or the paper she is using.

Lighting is also an important factor – she'd happily sit in a slowly darkening room rather than make the effort either to ask you to switch the light on for her or to switch it on herself. Remind her that she is able to see her toys more clearly when there is good lighting. And if one area of the room is brighter than another, tell her to sit there when playing.

Hand–eye coordination involves vision too, of course, and she's now at the age when she can play challenging visual games. For instance, when you are out together, ask her to look for cars that are the same as yours or to tell you every time she sees a baby being pushed in a buggy. The object you choose for her to identify is unimportant, just as long as she has to use her vision to locate it. You can also practise this type of activity whilst in the supermarket by asking your child to find a particular item for you.

Below: You will find that with some direction from you and practice your 4-year-old will be able to point accurately at small objects within the room.

❖❖❖❖❖❖❖ Top ❖ Tips ❖❖❖❖❖❖❖

1. Practise copying. She can now copy more complicated patterns and shapes. Draw some ordinary shapes and a couple of irregular ones on paper, then ask her to copy them underneath on the same piece of paper.

2. Sand and water play. Mix up sand and water in a basin so that the mixture is thick and sticky. She enjoys rubbing her hands in this, squeezing the 'mud' out between her fingers; she can also do this in the nursery.

3. Play pointing games. Stand on one side of the room with your child. Tell her to select an object on the opposite side and to point to it without saying anything. You have to guess first time what she is pointing at.

4. Bake together. A child this age loves mixing ingredients together in a big bowl using a huge wooden spoon, rolling out the mixture flat, cutting it into shapes and then putting these into the oven to cook.

5. Develop her visual memory. Put five objects on a tray, such as a spoon, a cup, a small toy, a pencil and a hairbrush. Let her study them for a minute, cover them with a towel, and see how many items she remembers.

Q Why does my child make such strange faces when she concentrates hard while playing with very small toys?

A The chances are that you do the same when, for instance, you try to thread a needle. Her twisted facial expression simply helps her focus her attention more on the job in hand, that's all. As she gets older, she will do this less and less.

Q Although my child is under 4, she insists on trying to button her coat by herself. This ends in tears. What should I do?

A Work in partnership with her, not in opposition. For instance, you can pull each button most of the way through, leaving her to tug the last section into place. This way she will be delighted with her success, and confrontation is avoided.

🧸🚚 **Toys:** crayons, paints, pencils and paper, jigsaws, people play figures and toy buildings, construction bricks that join together

Stimulating Hand–Eye Coordination: 4 to 4½ Years

Your child's handwriting skills consolidate and develop further. He probably realizes that the infant class is not too far away and his pretend play may reflect this – he plays 'schools' with his pals or with his play figures. This sharpens his enthusiasm for writing and drawing. He wants to be like 'the older ones', so he tries hard to be independent with manual tasks.

GETTING DRESSED

Despite your child's best efforts, getting himself dressed may be too difficult. Help him become independent by making this job easier. There are several ways you can do this. Advise him to lay out his clothes the night before in a neatly ordered pile, with the first item at the top.

If he can't tell the front from the back of, say, his jumper, put a small white sticker on the front. Once he has put it on properly, he can remove the sticker. Show him how to put one item of clothing on completely before turning to the next one.

Suitable Suggestions

Look closely at the way your child holds a pencil. You may discover that he has an unusual grip or that he holds it too far from the lead-exposed end, making the challenge of writing more difficult than it need be.

The most effective and efficient way he can grip a pencil for writing purposes is to hold it firmly between his thumb and forefinger (using his normal pincer grip), and then to place his middle finger so that it supports the pencil from underneath – the thumb and two fingers beside it form a tripod with the pencil in the centre. The three digits should meet at a distance from the pencil tip of about 1–2cm.

If your child has been used to holding the pencil in a different way, he may find this grip uncomfortable at first. Don't worry, he'll very quickly get used to it. Explain why this way of holding the pencil is best (for instance, because it's held firmly in position,

Below: This little boy is demonstrating the best way to hold a pen – between thumb and forefinger with the middle finger supporting the pen.

Left: At 4 children can master games with simple rules like this block game – delicate movements are needed to remove bricks without the tower collapsing.

A lot depends on the size and width of his fingers. Some children struggle to hold a pencil properly because it is so thin compared to the spacing that naturally forms between their fingers – in that instance, grip is enhanced by attaching a small rubber triangular grip close to the top of the pencil.

Help him develop his organizational skills, too. For instance, suggest that he keeps the play desk in his bedroom neat and tidy, with all the items put away at the end of each day before he goes to bed. He should also stack his toys and games neatly in the bedroom cupboard. Basic tidying and sorting tasks that involve hand–eye coordination also teach him to organize himself and his workspace, a skill that will be extremely useful once he joins the infant class.

and because he makes a mark on the paper more easily), encourage him to persist, and check that he doesn't resort to his old style. Within a few minutes, he'll be delighted with the results, whether he copies letters, traces over shapes, colours in pictures or just doodles on a sketch pad.

✦✦✦✦✦✦ Top·Tips ✦✦✦✦✦✦

1. Let him play on a toy piano. True, this guarantees you'll have a noisy afternoon. However, striking the keys is good for his hands and fingers. He'll be pleased with the tune, even if you're not.

2. Expect him to be a tidier eater. You can reasonably expect him to use his cutlery neatly at mealtimes. Assuming your child takes his time while eating, most of the food should arrive in his mouth with less on the table.

3. Make his own book. Tell your child to cut up some sheets of paper, and then let him see you staple these together to make his own special book. He wants to fill the pages with drawing and writing.

4. Refine his personal hygiene. Supervise him when he cleans his teeth or brushes his hair. These challenging activities should be easier for him now, but be prepared to guide him if you discover he doesn't do them properly.

5. Allow lots of water play. Fill a bowl with water and drop in two measuring jugs, one smaller than the other. Ask your child to fill the small one and then to pour it into the larger one without spilling a drop.

Below: Children of this age group love the responsibility of helping in the kitchen – and pouring, mixing, stirring and measuring all help with their motor skills.

Q My child insists on gripping the crayon with his palm, not his fingers. How can I change this?

A He does this because a palmar grip enables him to make a firm mark on the paper, whereas the proper finger grip is more challenging – gentle persuasion is therefore required. Demonstrate how the finger grip gives more control, softly encourage him to try this occasionally and point out how much better his drawings are when he holds the crayon in the proper way.

Q What can I do to improve my child's cutting skills with scissors?

A Give him a variety of cutting exercises, such as cutting a piece of paper into any number of pieces, cutting the corners off an oblong, cutting paper from one side through to the other, or cutting around a shape drawn on paper. He benefits from regular practice of this sort.

Toys: multiple-piece jigsaw puzzles, small construction bricks, colouring books and crayons, finger puppets, toy tool kit, peg board

Stimulating Hand–Eye Coordination: 4½ to 5 Years

In these final few months before your child starts school, her hand–eye coordination has reached the stage where she can probably write her first name without needing to copy it. Her hand control and pencil control still has a long way to go and you will continue to notice improvement over the next few years, yet the foundation of writing skills is firmly established.

In addition, your child has to understand that writing goes in one direction only (from left to right), that words contain lots of individual letters instead of one large pattern, and that a slightly different combination of the same shapes forms a completely different letter. No wonder, then, that few 5-year-olds write clearly!

Suitable Suggestions

Remember not to focus exclusively on encouraging your child to write, or she will soon get bored – and this could de-motivate her by the time she starts the infant class. There are many other ways to boost hand–eye coordination, all of which indirectly improve her writing potential. For instance, make up (or buy) a little book of mazes: each maze should consist of two parallel zigzagging lines roughly a centimetre apart, and the requirement is for your child to draw a line while keeping the tip of the pencil inside the lines of the maze. This isn't easy for a child aged 5 years whose hand is perspiring and trembling with excitement. If she tries to progress through the maze too slowly or too quickly, the line she draws will be erratic. Don't expect her to keep the pencil within the lines all the time. Playing this game makes her concentrate hard on her hand and eye movements.

Right: By now your child will be able to visualize and construct more complicated structures like buildings and bridges.

Drawing shapes and lines in sand is another suitable activity. Fill a flat plastic basin, or a tea tray that has raised edges, with silvery sand. Keep water away from it so that it remains dry all the time. Ask your child to use her index finger to draw, say, a circle in the sand. Once she has drawn various shapes and smooths the sand again each time, she can start to draw the letters of her name.

She continues to enjoy jigsaws, though she is now able to use a planned strategy instead of relying on luck to get a match between the pieces. Give her advice on this. For instance,

Above: Children of this age group are able to approach jigsaws in a less random way, identifying which areas they want to complete first.

◆◆◆◆◆◆◆ Top·Tips ◆◆◆◆◆◆◆

1. Involve her in cooking. She will thoroughly enjoy helping you by stirring various food mixtures with a spoon, or smoothing out a piece of pastry with a rolling pin. Even adding seasoning to food involves controlled hand–eye coordination skills.

2. Expect better use of cutlery. By the time she is 5 years old, your child can make a good attempt at eating with a fork and knife (although she probably prefers just to use a fork in her dominant hand). Give her encouragement.

3. Suggest more complex constructions. Now when she plays with construction blocks that link to each other, ask her to build a larger structure such as a small building, a car or a bridge. She is ready to tackle more demanding challenges.

4. Teach her to stack her clothes neatly. She might do this already, but if not, show her how to pile her clothes carefully so that they don't get crushed. Your child can't always fold them neatly but ask her to make an effort.

5. Show her how to wash her hands properly. Demonstrate that effective hand washing involves both hands rubbed together and that the fingers should also interlock while covered in water. She should also be able to dry her hands.

you could suggest that she finds the four corners first of all, followed by all the straight-edged pieces. Once she joins these bits together properly, she can fill the inside area. Or she could select the main object in the picture and identify all the pieces of that. The actual strategy doesn't matter so much as the fact that she uses her hand control in a planned way in order to achieve her target. This ability is extremely useful for all assignments in the infant class.

Below: This type of electronic maze will provide your child with a real challenge and he will need all his concentration to complete it successfully.

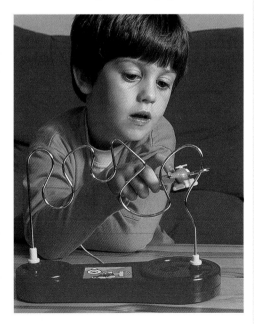

Q How can I help my 5-year-old form letters of the alphabet?

A Encourage her to make lots of writing patterns involving circles, wavy lines and straight lines. Start each pattern yourself and then ask her to complete the line. In addition, you could write her name in large letters at the top of a blank piece of paper and ask her to copy them underneath (or to trace them). Eventually, she will be able to write her name from scratch without copying.

Q Which letters should my child learn to write first?

A This varies from child to child. However, you will probably find that those letters involving either curves only (for example, 'c' and 'o') or straight lines only (for example, 't' and 'l') are rather easier for your child to learn than letters that involve combinations of lines and curves (for instance, 'b' and 'q').

Toys: pencils, crayons, colouring books, dot-to-dot books, child-sized scissors, jigsaws, plastic tool set, chalk and board, plastic utensils

Language

The Progress of Language

Your child uses language in ever more sophisticated ways during this phase of his life. This occurs partly through a better grasp of the rules of language, partly through his increased vocabulary and partly through his better learning skills. He starts to use language not just to communicate his own needs, but also to listen to the feelings and views of others. His sentences become longer, with a more complicated grammatical structure, and they carry more meaning, too. The typical 5-year-old can make a good contribution to any conversation with other children and adults.

Listening Skills

Now that he has a grasp of the fundamental elements of language, he builds on this by listening attentively to others – he learns a great deal about language just by focusing on what others say. But these skills vary from child to child.

You can help your child to sharpen his ability to tune in to what others say. Bear in mind that young children are frequently impulsive, preferring to spend more time doing exactly what they want to do instead of listening to someone else. That's why he may need additional help to develop listening skills. One of the most effective ways to achieve this is by reducing distractions. For example, he won't listen to what you say if you shout your message across the room while the television is blaring loudly beside him. Turn off the television before you speak to him, and remove other distractions if possible.

You may find that by the time he gives you his full attention he has missed the first part of your comments. To avoid this, say your child's name at the start of your sentence and only speak to him again when you are sure he is listening to you. Encourage him to make eye contact while you speak to him. If you think your child hasn't listened properly to you, ask him to repeat your instruction. Do this gently, not as a form of confrontation, but as a way to help him acquire good listening skills by the time he starts attending the infant class.

Reading

Some children aged 4 and 5 years spontaneously learn to read without any instruction from anyone. Just by looking and listening, they pick up the basic elements. Others need to be taught reading skills, however, and this is given full prominence in every infant class curriculum. But you don't need to wait until your child sets foot in school before he begins to learn to read – there is lots you can do to start the process.

You know that there is a direct connection between spoken language and written language: that what is written on paper is simply somebody's thoughts. Your growing child doesn't necessarily see the connection, so point it out to him. Use the written words that are all around him, those words that are part of his vocabulary already. For instance, he knows the name of his local supermarket – the next time you go there, show him the sign above the entrance and read the name to him.

Right: Reading books with your child is one of the most effective ways to stimulate language and an enthusiasm for words.

Above: At 5 years of age this girl has the vocabulary to carry out a detailed pretend shop transaction – from naming her purchases to asking for change.

Do the same with the wrappers that bear the name of his favourite sweets, or the carton that contains the name of his favourite video. Basic activities like these help him to see that reading is connected to everyday language, that it isn't something special just for school. He'll love cutting out the words from labels of products with which he is familiar.

And give him plenty of books to look at, even though he hasn't a clue about the individual words themselves. At the age of 3 years, your child can begin to understand that a book's title appears on the front page, that it is written by the author, that it needs to be held in a specific orientation for reading purposes, and that it starts at the front and finishes at the back. These facts are obvious to you, but not to your child. Understanding the nature of books is a fundamental pre-reading skill and it will also fire his enthusiasm.

Looking at comic books with your child is yet another source of language stimulation. He also loves those books that hide words and pictures under flaps.

The Art of Conversation

Your child is now more familiar with the concept of conversation – with the idea that he speaks, then the other person speaks, then he speaks again, and so forth. It is through this form of language interaction that he consolidates and improves his verbal skills, and therefore it is important that he is given plenty of opportunities for a two-way dialogue.

Make sure that you chat to him every day. Ask him simple questions about himself, his ideas and his feelings. Of course, he may not have much to say and would rather continue playing than talk to you at that particular moment. But chat to him anyway. Listen to what he has to say, even though it might appear trivial and repetitive. Your interest in his spoken words encourages him greatly.

Family life is often hectic, and at the end of a hard day a child aged 3, 4 or 5 years may not be able to get a word in because all those older than him – and therefore more fluent in spoken language – speak first and talk louder! Give your growing child space and time to speak.

Above: When you pick your child up from school or nursery, ask her about her day. Your interest encourages her to speak and she will enjoy telling you what she has done.

Below: At 2½ this little girl is chattering happily to herself as she plays.

Language

Age	Skill
2½–3 years	Your child is able to use literally hundreds of different words in her everyday speech, perhaps even more than a thousand. She combines them into sentences.
	She has discovered that questions are a good way to get your attention and also to gather information. She asks mainly 'Who?' and 'Where?' questions.
	Her previous tendency to use 'baby' speech has almost disappeared. One of the signs of her linguistic maturity is that she uses pronouns such as 'I' and 'he' appropriately and consistently.
3–3½ years	Sentence length increases. She no longer uses the minimum number of words to convey meaning but instead uses four or five words combined together.
	She now uses adjectives to describe everyday objects or people in her life. At this stage, though, she only uses two or three regularly but this steadily increases.
	She loves listening to stories, only now she becomes more involved, perhaps discussing it with you as you read to her. She likes to look at the book with you.
3½–4 years	Your child grasps basic language rules and uses them in her everyday speech; she is also able to apply them in a consistent, logical way to new words.
	She increases the length of her sentences by using 'and' as a link. However, she probably does this too often, making sentences uncomfortably long for the listener.

From 2½ to 5 Years

What to Do

Make a specific point of listening to her vocabulary over a period of two or three days. You may be surprised by the range of words she uses in conversation with you and her pals. You hear her talking so often you probably don't notice the progress.

Be patient with her never-ending questions: she likes to ask the same ones over and over again. And if she doesn't ask enough questions, do your best to encourage her to do so – explain to your child that she should ask if she is uncertain.

You'll find that she starts to say things like 'I want' instead of 'me want', and 'he did' instead of 'James did'. When she uses a pronoun incorrectly, as she inevitably will do at times, don't make fun of her or correct her. Instead, say the phrase properly.

Chat to her as a matter of routine, no matter what you are doing. She will naturally extend the length of sentences she uses, as long as you provide a good model for her to copy. Your child's language structures begin to resemble your own.

Use basic adjectives yourself when talking to her, such as 'big', 'little', 'happy' and 'sad'. You'll find that she starts to use them more frequently too. Prepositions such as 'in', 'under' and 'over' start to appear in her spoken vocabulary.

When you read a story to her, sit together, side by side, so that she can look at each page clearly. Point to the accompanying pictures as they are mentioned in the story. Encourage your child to ask questions, and ask her about the story when you have finished.

On the left side of a piece of paper, draw a shape; on the right side, draw the same shape three times. Point to the single shape and say 'Here is a nid', then point to the three shapes and say 'Here are....' She'll say 'nids', showing that she understands how to make plurals.

By all means let her use conjunctions such as 'and' or 'but' because this helps her expressive ability. However, if you find that she uses several 'ands' in a row, encourage her to keep her sentences shorter by only using one or two conjunctions at most.

Language

Age	Skill

She realizes that language can be used to improve her learning, not just to express her feelings, and so she starts to ask you difficult 'How?' and 'Why?' questions.

4–4½ years

Your child is able to give you a reasonably accurate account of a recent experience, perhaps something that happened to her at nursery earlier that day or a video she watched.

Nursery rhymes, songs and poems are very important in your child's life. She likes to recite familiar rhymes to you, and actively joins in as many songs as possible.

She has a clearer idea of the names of the main primary colours and is able to identify them accurately, either as a matching activity or in response to a question.

4½–5 years

By now her spoken vocabulary is so extensive that you couldn't possibly count all the words even if you tried – she probably uses at least several thousand different words.

Most children starting school are able to give accurate biographical details to an adult who asks appropriate questions. She is confident enough to give a correct reply.

In many ways, her speech and language patterns more closely resemble those of an adult than those of a younger child. She talks more maturely and coherently.

From 2½ to 5 Years

What to Do

Be prepared to take these enquiries seriously. Her improved thinking skills prompt her to seek more detailed information from you in order to help her make sense of the world. Answer these challenging enquiries as best you can.

When you collect her from nursery or from playing with a friend, ask her what she did, what games she played, and so on. She can provide you with a description that leaves you with a rough impression of what went on while she was there.

Sing lots of songs with her, choosing new as well as familiar ones. Encourage her to learn the words so that she can sing them on her own. She loves you to read her favourite poems. If she feels confident, she'll recite short rhymes to others

Put out a number of plastic blocks which are coloured red, yellow, blue and green. Ask your child to make a pile of the yellow blocks – she does this without asking for any help. And she can do the same for each of these bright colours.

When you have a conversation with your child, encourage her to use a broad range from her vocabulary. If she tends to use the same words all the time, suggest ways she can say the same thing differently. She follows your advice.

Teach your child basic details about herself, such as her name, address, date of birth and telephone number. Give her time to learn all this information, which she may find challenging at first. Practise this each day as the start to infant school draws near.

Your child has clear views and she likes to tell you about them. Listen carefully, then reply – whether agreeing or disagreeing – and ask her questions. Surround her with interesting books, tell her lots of exciting stories and sing lots of songs together.

Stimulating Language: 2½ to 3 Years

Your child's speech and language become more complex at this point in his life because he has a broader vocabulary, a greater understanding of grammar and an increased confidence in using language to express his needs. If he is excited or agitated, he gets confused and his words may be jumbled. In most instances, however, he can make himself understood to you.

AT HIS OWN PACE

There are huge variations in the rate at which children learn language skills. There are also gender differences: for instance, girls generally learn to speak at an earlier age than boys. Many parents worry because their 3-year-old doesn't use complex sentences like the child next door of the same age, but such concerns are usually unnecessary.

Rather than focusing your attention on any perceived weaknesses in your child's speech, give him lots of language stimulation – that's the best way to boost his progress. If you concentrate on something he can't say properly, this could make him anxious. Your child develops at his own pace, in his own time.

Suitable Suggestions

Your child thoroughly enjoys action rhymes at this stage because these allow him to demonstrate his skills in different areas. For instance, reciting 'I'm a little teapot' involves memory, language and coordination skills. Don't worry if your child repeats the same rhymes and poems every day – repetition helps him remember the lines and builds up his awareness that some words share the same ending. Try him with tongue-twister rhymes as they enhance his pronunciation skills, though don't expect him to give a faultless performance!

Nursery experience broadens his use of language. Until now, he has primarily spoken to you or his siblings, all of whom are able to tune in easily to what he has to say. At nursery, he mixes with other children who are not so familiar to him, and they too are developing their speech. This means that your child has to work harder to make his needs understood. He also learns from the speech and language of other children.

Expect your child to make mistakes with language. He's still learning and at times uses the wrong word in the wrong place or maybe uses an immature style of speech. Errors like this are perfectly normal and nothing to be concerned about. Instead of correcting each

mistake, just say the right form to him as if confirming what he has said. For instance, if he tells you that 'Me wented to the bathroom', you could reply 'That's good, you went to the bathroom.' He'll pick up the correct phrasing from you.

Play with your child and talk to him about his toys – he's more likely to use the full scope of his language potential when the topic of conversation is one that fascinates him. Ask him to tell you which is his favourite toy and the games he likes to play with it. This will naturally lead him on to talk about his other toys, and then you can

Below: If you maintain eye contact with your child while you are talking to him he will concentrate more on what you are saying.

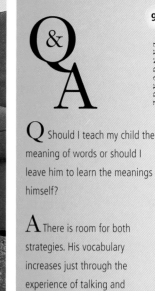

Q Should I teach my child the meaning of words or should I leave him to learn the meanings himself?

A There is room for both strategies. His vocabulary increases just through the experience of talking and listening to you, or from mixing with his friends. However, you can also teach him words that he may find useful; he learns nouns more easily than adjectives or verbs.

Q When my 3-year-old plays with a puzzle toy he talks to himself. Why?

A This is known as 'self-directing' speech because your child gives himself spoken instructions on how to complete the puzzle. In other words, he uses language to guide himself to the correct solution. Many adults do the same, except that they think the words instead of saying them out loud.

Toys: story books, dolls and soft toys, song tapes, musical instruments, plastic kitchen equipment, doll's tea set

❖❖❖❖❖❖❖ Top ❖ Tips ❖❖❖❖❖❖❖

1. Don't chuckle at his mistakes. Sometimes his language contains mistakes which appear cute to an adult. Yet drawing attention to these errors makes him very self-conscious, possibly making him reluctant to talk so openly in the future.

2. Play a game involving sound recognition. Take him for a short walk outside. Stand still, and then while holding his hand securely, tell him to shut his eyes. Ask him to identify the sounds that he hears around him – for instance, a car driving past or a bird singing.

3. Talk to him about television programmes. He is bound to watch television or a video at least for a few minutes on some days. Once he has stopped watching, ask him questions about the programme's content, and what he liked about it.

4. Say a familiar rhyme but don't complete it. Once you are sure that he knows a particular rhyme, miss out the last word of each line and look at him in expectation, so that he supplies the missing word. He enjoys this word game.

5. Encourage eye contact during conversation. His attention is greater when he looks you in the eye as you talk to each other. Discourage him from doing something else while you chat together.

Above: Interaction with other children plays an important part in improving your child's conversational skills.

broaden out the discussion in any direction you like. What matters is that he begins to understand that language has a social purpose, too – that it is a way of cementing personal relationships.

Below: Asking your child to identify a sound with his eyes shut helps him to draw upon his vocabulary without a visual prompt.

Stimulating Language: 3 to 3½ Years

Progress in language continues as your child is more animated in her use of words, phrases and sentences. She enjoys talking – even when you would rather have some peace and quiet – and is happy to tell you all her news. She combines words, gestures and facial expressions to make her accounts vivid and interesting. Her words flow more easily, with less effort.

BODY LANGUAGE

Although your child's spoken language skills improve, she still uses body language to convey meaning. Pay attention to her facial expressions, hand and arm gestures, breathing and posture, all of which tell you something about her feelings. By now you are probably skilled in interpreting these indicators.

One of the useful aspects of non-verbal communication is that it is harder to control than spoken words because most of it is involuntary, without any underlying planning – as a result, it can give you a more accurate impression of your child's feelings. This is particularly helpful when she won't express her emotions verbally.

Suitable Suggestions

There may be times when you collect your child from nursery or playgroup, or perhaps a friend's house, only to discover that she is quiet and reflective. She simply doesn't feel like chatting to you. That's fine and should not become a source of confrontation between you. It could be that she is tired from her long day, or maybe she has fallen

Below: As children play together they will often describe to each other what they are doing in their game.

out with a friend and is in a bad mood. Whatever the cause of her reluctance to chat, give her space. She'll return to her usual talkative self within the next hour or so if you just leave her alone.

Use people and animal play figures to stimulate her language. Suggest to your child that she makes a farm scene using these figures, toy farm buildings and fences. Once she has done that, ask her to give you a 'guided tour' of the farm, explaining who the people are and what they do on the farm.

You'll be surprised at the extent of her imagination and the sorts of information she gives you about her pretend play sequence. Look interested, make positive remarks and pose questions to her on the basis of comments she makes.

When you take her with you on a shopping trip to your local supermarket, as you reach the door point to the name of the store in the sign above and let her stare at it for a few moments. When you get home, cut out the store logo and name from the plastic carrier bag and paste it into a little book of blank pages for her. You could also do this with the logo of her

Above: By the age of 3 your child will be able to follow an instruction that you give her involving two or three consecutive actions.

favourite breakfast cereal, putting one on each of the blank pages.

The next time you return to the store, tell your child to bring the book with her. She has to let you know when she sees the name logo anywhere throughout the supermarket – put a tick in her book as a reward. This game uses print images in her environment to build her basic word recognition skills even though she can't read individual letters yet.

Below: Make-believe games with toy characters encourage your child to use language in a creative and imaginative way.

Q & A

Q My 3½-year-old has trouble saying some sounds, such as 'th' and 'sm'. What should I do?

A This is a common occurrence, which you don't need to do anything about. Many children this age experience temporary difficulty with double-letter blends like these – for instance, substituting 'f' for 'th'. However, this self-corrects over the next few months as her pronunciation in general improves.

Q Why is my 3½-year-old so quiet at nursery? She prattles away non-stop at home.

A You know from her talkative nature at home that she can speak fluently and appropriately. Her silence at nursery probably arises because she is not yet fully at ease with the other children and adults. Her use of language there will steadily increase as she begins to feel more comfortable.

Toys: finger puppets, dressing-up clothes, doll's house and furniture, story books, magazines and newspapers to cut up

✦✦✦✦✦✦✦ Top·Tips ✦✦✦✦✦✦✦

1. **Give more complicated instructions.** Make a request that contains two or three pieces of information, for example: 'Go into the kitchen and bring me the blue cloth.' If she concentrates on what you say, she is able to complete the task.

2. **Sing songs together.** Your child enjoys singing even more now that she is able to learn and remember the words. Take a musical tape or CD with you for car journeys. This relieves the boredom and improves her language skills.

3. **Play puppet games.** Encourage her to play imaginatively with her finger puppets so that they talk to each other or to you. Some children use more language in this play format than they usually do in everyday life.

4. **List 'sounds like' words.** This isn't easy, but she might manage. Say a couple of words that rhyme (such as 'cat' and 'mat'), making sure that you stress the end sound. Then ask her to suggest other words that sound like these. Most children find this harder than finding words with the same starting sound.

5. **Play listening games.** With her eyes closed while listening to a video or television programme with which she is familiar, ask her to identify the different voices she hears. The chances are that her guesses are accurate.

Stimulating Language: 3½ to 4 Years

As he approaches his fourth birthday, your child starts to use language more creatively and more purposefully. His questions are more penetrating as he seeks more detailed information. He also applies the rules of grammar himself, though he doesn't always do this correctly – that's why you might hear him tell you that his friend 'gonded' instead of 'went'. His sentences are longer.

HEARING DIFFICULTIES

Hearing loss is the most common reason for a child's slow progress with speech and language development. Although problems with hearing are usually picked up in the first couple of years, there are some children whose difficulty isn't identified until later.

Signs of possible hearing loss in a child this age include his slower than expected progress with speech, a lack of response to questions, his habit of watching the speaker's face and mouth closely, and a high level of frustration. These signs by themselves don't necessarily mean he has hearing loss, but if you have any doubts, check this out.

Suitable Suggestions

As well as generally chatting to your child, ask him questions that require him to think about a topic and then to respond to you. For instance, you could ask him to tell you what it is about his favourite cuddly toy that he likes so much, or why he prefers playing with one child rather than another. He is ready to cope with this level of discussion, but may need your prodding to get him going. When you have had a good chat, tell him how much you enjoyed talking to him.

You'll also find that his humour shows through, although he'll burst out laughing at something that doesn't even make you smile! At this age, much of his humour revolves around language. Your child might say a word out of context, then roll around on the floor with laughter – you may not see what is so funny, but he thinks he has made a hilarious joke. Just go along with his verbal humour: don't ask him to explain it to you. He'll also like stories involving characters with funny names who say strange things to others in the story. This is a sign of his ability to go beyond a literal understanding of the spoken word.

It's important that your child feels that you listen to him. If possible, stop what you are doing and give him your full attention. If you

Above: At this age your child will love the novelty of a walkie-talkie toy – this is likely to enthral even the most reluctant talker.

can't do this because you are particularly busy, tell him this and explain that you'll listen to him in a few minutes when you have some time. And make sure you do seek his views later on or he'll soon stop making the effort to talk to you.

Q I don't read fairy tales to my 4-year-old because I think they are frightening. Am I right?

A Fairy tales can be scary for young children, but it depends on the way you read them. If you use a voice tone that makes him nervous, he will be frightened. But if you use a pleasant voice, filled with excitement, then he'll probably enjoy listening to these tales.

Q Why has my child started to develop a lisp? He says 'th' instead of 's'.

A This type of sound substitution is normal, and often happens around the age of 3 or 4 years. In virtually all instances, the lisp disappears as the child matures, usually before he sets foot in the infant class. He may feel self-conscious, so don't draw attention to it.

Toys: reading books, picture cards with lots of details, magazines, magnetic letters and board, nursery rhyme books

✦✦✦✦✦✦✦ Top ✦ Tips ✦✦✦✦✦✦✦

1. Talk about holiday photographs. Get out the pictures you took during your previous family holiday and chat about them with your child. Let him look at them, ask him to point out the various details and tell you what he recalls about the trip.

2. Use magnetic letters. Initially, use these for letter-matching games. Draw a letter on paper, hand it to your child and ask him to find the magnetic letter that is the same. Vary the complexity of this.

3. Play word lotto. The chances are that he can't read any of the words on the lotto board, but he may be able to match the cards with them if given enough time to compare them. Pick cards with words containing only two or three letters.

4. Teach him poetry. Encourage him to learn a poem containing only, say, two lines. Rehearse this with him until he is reasonably confident. The next time relatives visit, suggest he recites the poem to them.

5. Ask him to describe flavours. Give your child four different items to taste and ask him to describe their flavours. Tell him you don't know which one he has tasted so he needs to try hard to give you a clear description, such as 'nice' or 'horrible'.

Above: Magnetic letters on a board or the fridge are a great means of familiarizing your child with the alphabet.

Some children this age start to stammer when they speak while excited. It's as if they are so desperate to get the words out quickly that they jumble them up. Encourage him to talk more slowly. Speak to him in a quiet, steady voice, reminding him to slow down and to take a breath at the end of each sentence. With your advice and support, this temporary speech mannerism will pass.

Below: Children love looking through photo albums and talking about the pictures, particularly those of events that they remember.

Stimulating Language: 4 to 4½ Years

Your child's better use of language enables her to deal with more complex thoughts. Many of the pre-school language skills emerge now, such as identifying and naming colours and shapes. This boosts her confidence, curiosity and desire to know more – so her questions increase, too. She chats freely to other children at every opportunity, and likes to voice her opinions.

REPETITIVE READING

Most children this age love to hear the same story over and over again. To you this may appear to be a dreadfully boring and pointless exercise, but to your 4½-year-old it is fascinating. He loves the familiarity and predictability of the story because it is reassuring and comforting.

Repetition of stories like this also improves his language development – you'll find that he starts to mouth the words as you read, or maybe even says the next line of the story before you do. Of course, as well as reading familiar stories to your child, you should gradually introduce new ones, too.

Suitable Suggestions

Listening is an essential part of communication. Your 4-year-old, however, may be more intent on expressing her own point of view (loudly) – especially when she is driven by righteous indignation – than she is on listening. When she feels hard done by, she is determined to let you know. It's best to let her have her say (whether you agree with her or not), while you listen calmly. When she has finished, take your turn. Tell her that you have listened to what she said and ask

Below: Your child will now sing confidently and can accompany himself on instruments; get him to make up words for a familiar tune or invent new songs.

Left: These two boys are trying to identify different smells – this is an excellent way to get them to stretch their descriptive vocabulary.

her to listen to you now. Then say what you think about the matter.

You may find that your child simply repeats what she said the first time, as if in the hope that repetition will ensure she wins the argument. Each time she does this, repeat the point you made and ask her to reply to that specific comment. Slowly but surely, you'll help her transform from a determined 4-year-old who aims to win an argument by verbal force into a sensitive child who listens to the other person.

This is also a good time to explain to her about the power of language, that words can cheer up another person or can make them unhappy: in other words, that her speech and language have an emotional impact on others. She probably makes hurtful comments completely unintentionally – she simply says what enters her mind at this age, without giving a thought to the potential consequences to those she's talking to.

For instance, when she sees another child who looks different from her, she may say 'You look funny', perhaps because of that child's haircut or the clothes he wears. She doesn't realize that her remark could cause upset. You can broaden her perspective by asking her to tell you how she would feel if someone made that comment to her. Point out that others feel the same way as well.

Books should occupy part of her daily routine now. She probably points to some of the words as she sits beside you while you read to her, and she may pick out letters that are included in her name. Playing with magnetic letters and a board builds her emerging reading skills.

✦✦✦✦✦✦ Top·Tips ✦✦✦✦✦✦

1. Discuss recent experiences. No matter what she has done that day, make sure that you ask her about it. Get her into the habit of giving you a good account of her experiences, whether she was at nursery or played at home.

2. Select her television viewing carefully. Since her language is influenced by what she sees on television, do your best to ensure that she watches quality children's programmes that are made specifically for young viewers.

3. Encourage letter recognition. Instead of asking her to pick out her name from, say, six names that you write on paper, just write the first letters of the names. Ask her to pick out the letter that starts her own name.

4. Use verbal humour with her. She begins to see that there are additional humorous aspects to language, such as gentle sarcasm. For instance, when she spills something, smile as you say 'That's good, isn't it'. Your child understands the joke.

5. Play 'I spy'. Ask her to identify objects starting with a specific sound, such as 'p' or 'm'. Vary this by making the starting sounds a two-letter combination, such as 'st' or 'tr'. Help your child if she struggles to do this.

Q Which should come first, naming shapes or identifying them?

A Your child will be able to pick out specific shapes when requested long before she can actually tell you the name of each shape. In most instances, a child's receptive language (the words she can understand) is ahead of her expressive language (the words she can say), and so shape and colour identification emerges before naming.

Q Whenever my child hears a new word, she says it over and over again. Why?

A Put simply, she finds words fascinating. To you, word repetition is boring, but to your child, this is a great game. Just leave her to it. Once she has integrated the word into her vocabulary, she won't need to use it so often.

Toys: people and animal play figures, lots of books, magnetic letters and numbers, coloured shapes, dressing-up hats

Stimulating Language: 4½ to 5 years

Language has become your child's elementary tool for learning – he understands the importance of books and looks at factual books, not just fiction. He also uses language as a key social skill. When he was younger, he acted first and then asked permission; now it's usually the other way around. Your child is confident talking to an adult and can answer personal questions.

VERBAL POLITENESS

Politeness with words does matter, to both children and adults. A child who is able to say, for example, 'please' and 'thank you' is far more likely to keep his friends than a child who just grabs at what he wants without saying a word. Although most children this age act on impulse, it's best if he can learn basic verbal politeness before starting the infant class.

Set a good example at home. Gently but firmly insist that he asks appropriately for a sweet, toy or game instead of barging his way through, and don't give him what he wants unless he asks nicely. This use of language makes life easier for him.

Suitable Suggestions

You can enhance your child's social use of language by teaching him opening gambits to use when meeting new children for the first time, as he will do when he starts the infant class. Children are often shy when mixing with others they don't know well, and this results in their not knowing what to say.

To help your child have an easier social start to school, suggest to him that he says, for example, 'Would you like to play with my toy?' or 'I like jumping. Would you like to play with me?' or 'That's a nice jumper you're wearing.' He may feel silly practising these sentences at home with you, but he'll understand their social purpose.

Encourage him to be confident when asking questions. This is crucial for the infant school, not just to acquire knowledge in the classroom but also for personal issues as well. For instance, there are some children who fail to use the infant toilet in the first few weeks of starting school simply because they don't have the courage to ask the

Right: This little girl is taking the lead in a shopping game. Getting your child used to asking questions will help her at school.

teacher where it is located. And you don't want your child to fall into that trap about any question he needs to ask.

Get him used to asking you for things, instead of anticipating his requests. He could also, for instance ask the local shopkeeper for an item (in your presence, of course). The more he does this, the more confident he becomes with questions. Remind him that he should only ask when he genuinely needs to know something, not to

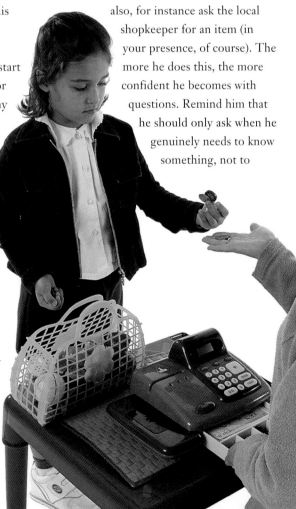

Above: If you teach your child some basic ways to open a conversation he will feel more confident when meeting new people.

✦✦✦✦✦✦✦ Top·Tips ✦✦✦✦✦✦✦

1. Use print in his surroundings. Draw his attention to road and shop signs, all of which carry important information. Explain what each sign tells you and encourage him to identify the starting letter.

2. Give him blank paper and pencils for writing. It's important for your child to realize that he can write the words that he says. Help him note down a short sentence that he has spoken to you, and then read it back to him.

3. Put up labels. You could put labels on key objects around your house, such as the table, chair, door and television. Don't do this for everything – just for, say, half a dozen basic items. He'll soon be able to read these labels out of context.

4. Include him in conversations. If your child is quiet by nature, he may prefer to take a backseat role when others talk. Make a point of including him in your conversations, irrespective of his possible reluctance to speak.

5. Use lettering of different sizes, type style and case (capital and small letters). Instead of looking for reading books with the same size and style of print, give your child a variety. That's better than uniformity because it gets him used to a broad range of print.

make himself the centre of attention. With your guidance, he'll strike a balance.

By now he should be immersed in reading books, magazines, newspapers and comics, as well as his own made-up books. Take him to your local library each week. Make a point of reading together each day, and ask him lots of questions about the characters and the plot, about what he thinks will happen next and about his enjoyment. You could even suggest that he writes a letter (with your help) to the story's central character.

Below: Once your child can read she will enjoy reading alone although many books she likes will still be too complex for her to read unaided.

Q Does a child this age understand the concept of a 'white lie'?

A A white lie (a lie whose purpose is to protect another person's feelings) can confuse a 5-year-old. He may not realize the difference between this type of lie and an unacceptable lie to conceal the truth. If he hears you tell a white lie, he may take this as a sign that lying is permissible.

Q What is phonological awareness?

A This is an important language skill, and is your child's ability to understand that a whole word such as 'cat' can be broken into the segments 'c' and 'at'. There is evidence that a child who grasps this idea by the age of 4 or 5 years is likely to make good progress with reading in the infant class.

Toys: puppets and dolls, musical tapes, books, newspapers, clothes for imaginative play, word lotto, board games

Learning

The Development of Learning Skills

Your child's learning ability (also called 'intelligence', 'learning skills', 'thinking skills' and 'cognition') continues to grow rapidly during these remaining pre-school years. Her ability to learn new skills and concepts, to make sense of events that happen around her, to use her memory accurately and to solve problems steadily improves.

An Active Thinker

By the time she reaches her fifth birthday, your child is a much more active thinker, with a great deal more knowledge and grasp of concepts than she had a few years earlier. Look for changes in the following areas:

• **concentration.** She is now able to focus her attention more accurately and is less influenced by distractions; she blocks out irrelevant information in order to concentrate on the item or object that catches her interest. This skill is particularly important in the infant classroom, where she will need to concentrate on one activity only while a lot goes on around her.

• **inquisitiveness.** Your child has an innate curiosity that drives her to learn more and more. There is so much she wants to understand, and the intensity of her questioning increases. She also learns by hands-on discovery herself – physical exploration remains a key strategy for enhancing her learning, though she approaches such activities in a more organized way now.

• **number concepts.** Genuine understanding of the significance of numbers begins to emerge around the third and fourth year. Initially, she tries to count in imitation –

without understanding the meaning of numbers – but then she starts to match small groups with the same number of objects in them. This is a huge step forward in her ability to deal with abstract concepts.

• **memory.** Her increasing memory skills underpin much of her learning – if her memory was weak, she wouldn't recall what she had learned the previous day and would have to re-learn it all over again. Now she

can hold two or three pieces of information in her memory while she acts on them. Her short- and long-term memories both show signs of increased capacity.

• **symbolic thought.** She starts to use imagery as part of her thinking. She is more able to discuss people,

Below: By the time your child is 3½ her concentration increases, allowing her to complete tasks like a dot-to-dot puzzle.

objects and toys that aren't actually there in front of her at the time, so she is no longer tied to what she can see. This opens up a whole new range of learning opportunities. Imagery also enables her to generalize what she has learned from one situation to another.

Learning Style

By now, you'll have a good idea of the way in which your child approaches learning activities and her attitude towards them. Psychologists call this her 'learning style', and it is important because it affects her progress at school. Spend a moment or two observing your child play with a brand new toy. Perhaps she grabs at it, hurriedly takes it out of the box and then immediately tries to operate it. Or maybe she looks at the box and the toy first, as she tries to make sense of it before playing with it, and then slowly begins to play.

These two different approaches to acquiring information are known as:
• **impulsive.** With this learning style, a child acts before thinking the problem through properly. She is driven by impulse and instinct, heading for a solution that she guesses might be effective or that has worked in the past with a different problem. The impulsive

child doesn't wait to evaluate, but instead tries to solve the problem before weighing up all the possibilities.
• **reflective.** With this learning style, a child tends to think before she acts. She gathers as much information as she can about the challenge facing her before searching for a solution. When she thinks she is ready, she starts to apply some of that newly acquired data in a problem-solving strategy. Time is of no consequence to a child with a reflective learning style – she acts only when she feels ready.

You'll probably see elements of both learning styles in your child, and there is a place for each of these approaches when it comes to learning during the pre-school years. For instance, if your child takes too long to reach a decision about, say, the best biscuits to eat, other children may

Right: At 3 this little boy has his binoculars the wrong way round but he will soon realize this and try them the other way.

Above: Inquisitiveness, prior knowledge and logic enable these children to work out how to get biscuits from a high cupboard.

have finished them all by the time she makes up her mind. On the other hand, she is likely to have a safer childhood if, for instance, she studies the traffic pattern very carefully before crossing the road. Each style has merit, depending on the learning context.

Confidence with Learning

As your child's thinking skills increase, she inevitably tries more challenging learning activities. In some instances she will fail to achieve her learning target, whether that's completing a large jigsaw puzzle or learning the sequence of the first five numbers. This can depress her self-confidence, thus reducing her willingness to learn new information in the future. Do your best to keep her confidence as a learner high so that she maintains an upbeat, positive outlook about her learning skills.

Learning

Age	Skill
2½–3 years	Your child begins to understand that money is used to buy items, although he doesn't fully understand about the different coins and notes and how they are combined.

His ability to compare two objects using one characteristic emerges, although he gets confused at times. He can't compare them using two characteristics at the same time.

He has improved short- and long-term memory, which enables him to recall experiences that occurred recently and also those that took place months ago.

| 3–3½ years | Your child's drawing reflects his increased intellectual maturity. He is more able to portray his perceptions of the world on paper, though they are still very basic. |

Short-term memory advances to the extent that he may be able to hold new information for a few seconds and then report it back accurately to you.

He develops an elementary understanding of numbers because he hears and sees other people using them. But he doesn't know what each number means or signifies.

| 3½–4 years | He has probably reached the first stage of genuine counting. He likes the sounds of numbers and recites the number sequence to anyone who will listen to him. |

Your child uses his imagination to create an image that isn't actually in front of him. He is able to control that image and to tell you details about what he sees.

From 2½ to 5 Years

What to Do

Take a mix of coins in your hand and show them to your child. Ask what they are. He'll probably say 'money'. Don't expect him to be able to name the individual coins, however, or even to know that each coin has its own value.

Take two apples of different sizes from the fruit bowl. Place them both in front of your child and ask him to 'point to the bigger apple'. If you give him time to answer, he'll be able to select the right one. You can do this with other objects as well.

Ask your child to tell you about the game he just played – he can give you lots of information about it. Once you have done this, chat to him about the family holiday taken a few months ago. With prompts, he'll remember some of the main details.

Suggest to him that he draws a picture of you. The finished product will be recognizable as a person. However, you'll notice that the head is extremely large, with no body attached to it, and the legs stick out from underneath. He may put in the eyes.

Tell your child two single numbers, with a one-second gap between each number, and then immediately ask him to say these numbers back to you. Let him know in advance that this is what you want him to do. The chances are he'll remember both digits.

You can start to teach him the sequence of numbers up to, say, three. Don't try to associate each number with a quantity at this stage, because he is unlikely to grasp that notion fully at present, but he should be able to rote learn the sequence itself.

As well as being able to recite the numbers up to five, and possibly even beyond, he begins to associate numbers with objects. Put a row of small blocks in front of him and ask him to count as you point. He does this accurately up to the second or third block.

When he sits beside you with no other distractions, tell him to imagine a king and queen with lots of lovely clothes and jewels. Ask him to describe the scene to you. He'll stare in front as he lists aspects of the purely imaginary scene that he has created.

Learning

Age	Skill

His concentration and organizational skills improve, enabling him to make a more systematic search for something for which he is looking. He is more focused.

4–4½ years

Although he continues to make comparisons between two objects using only one characteristic at a time, he can make these judgements using a broader range of criteria.

Your child understands the difference between right and wrong but judges the morality of an action in terms of its consequences, not its intent.

He has an awareness of time, and that the day is split into sequences. He may also know that babies, animals and plants grow, and that an adult is older than a child. He might have discovered that pets can die, as can plants.

4½–5 years

Your child's concentration has matured. He is not so easily distracted and persists at an activity, without needing a break, until he is satisfied that it is finished.

His increased memory and better ability to organize himself mean that he is able to plan ahead, perhaps to make preparations for an activity that isn't going to happen until tomorrow.

Recognition and grasp of numbers has progressed, and he realizes that when counting a row of objects, one number goes with one item – he doesn't miss one out.

From 2½ to 5 Years

What to Do

Ask your child to find an object in his room, something that is reasonably easy to find. Advise him to look in the cupboard first, then in his toy box. You'll find that he does search systematically as you suggested, instead of poking about randomly.

Give him lots of comparisons to make, using different characteristics each time. For instance, he can compare two lumps of play-doh to decide which is fatter or thinner, and two pieces of fruit to decide which is heavier or lighter.

Tell him the following story: 'A young child deliberately splashed a small dab of paint on the wall, while his friend accidentally spilled lots of paint on the floor.' Ask him who was more wrong – he'll say it was the one who spilled lots of paint.

While he can't tell the time from a clock face, he knows, for instance, that the day starts with breakfast, dinner comes towards the end of the day, bedtime is at night, and so on. Ask him to tell you about the sequences in his day, and about what will happen next.

Show him a short video for five minutes or give him a small book to look through, and ask him to complete the activity without leaving his seat. If he does start to move out of position, remind him that he has to stay there until he finishes the task.

Help your child become a better planner by encouraging him to think ahead. When he anticipates an outing with you to, say, the park, ask him to think what he'll need to take with him so that he has everything. Encourage him to imagine all the possibilities.

Show him the written numbers from one to nine – he may already be able to recognize and name them. When asked to recite the numbers up to ten, he probably manages this comfortably, and he also counts objects accurately up to three or four.

Stimulating Learning: 2½ to 3 Years

Learning skills progress significantly during this period. You'll notice that your child is able to remember more information – both new and old – and she chats about things that happened to her a few days ago. She is able to grasp new concepts, such as money, height and length, and this helps her to make sense of the world around her.

MEMORY GAMES

Your child's memory skills are improved through practice and training, especially through games. You can make them up yourself. For instance, try this game. Group together a series of familiar objects with different textures, such as a slice of bread, a small book, a teaspoon, a cup, a vest and so on. Let your child handle these for a couple of minutes and then remove them. After ten minutes, place the objects in a bag and ask your child to guess what each object is just by touching it, without looking. She has great fun recalling as many items as she can.

Suitable Suggestions

Encourage her classification skills: in other words, her ability to sort items into groups. She does this intuitively already – for instance, she knows that she is a girl, that the things she sits on are chairs even though they are all different, that cats are different from dogs – but you can help to develop this further by providing her with sorting activities. Give her a pile of dolls mixed up with some wooden blocks, then ask her to put all the dolls in one pile and all the bricks in another. Provide variations of this activity.

Your child picks up new information simply from everyday experience. That's why it's important just to chat to her about what you

do, about the things going on around her and about her daily experiences. When you draw her attention to these, she looks more closely at them and considers them in more detail. This incidental, unplanned learning goes on all the time.

Bear in mind that at this age you can't possibly know the full extent of your child's learning potential – you certainly will have already formed an opinion about this, based on your knowledge of her over the last couple of years, but you have no idea how

Below: By 3, children have grasped the concept of relative size. This boy will understand that his snake is long rather than short and longer than his other toys.

Left: Playing with your child helps him to maintain his concentration on an activity for longer than if he plays alone.

accurate that view is. With some children, their true learning ability does not show through until later on in childhood, adolescence or even adulthood.

So have high expectations of your child. That doesn't mean you should push her to learn all the time, just that you should always provide opportunities which are challenging and which offer the chance to extend her knowledge and understanding.

Your child's concentration fluctuates, though in most instances it doesn't last very long. Since the ability to focus on an activity aids learning, encourage her to attend to a toy or game for a few more seconds. Do this with verbal prompts ('Play with the toy for a little longer') or by sitting with her as she plays – research shows that a child plays with a toy for longer when her parent is present.

Below: A toy cash register is a good way to introduce your child to money and the idea of prices, paying for things and giving change.

❖❖❖❖❖❖❖ Top·Tips ❖❖❖❖❖❖❖

1. Suggest that she repeats information. Her ability to memorize information improves when she repeats it. Once you have given her a basic instruction, ask her to say it back to you; this technique makes it more likely that she'll remember information that she's given.

2. Ask her to make up a story. Now that she has better imagination skills, she enjoys using them to create a fantasy story. Listen intently as she chats, and ask her questions about the people and places in her made-up tale.

3. Buy her a toy cash register. She doesn't understand the value of the coins but she has fun pretending to be a shopkeeper. Suggest she puts a price tag on a few items so that customers know what they can afford.

4. Provide model constructions for her to copy. Take six wooden blocks and build a bridge with them. Let your child look at it. Then give her the same number of blocks and ask her to make a bridge just like yours.

5. Remember to praise her successes. To your child, every achievement is a great delight – whether it is finding her toy without help or completing a larger jigsaw – and your approval adds to her pleasure. Give her lots of praise.

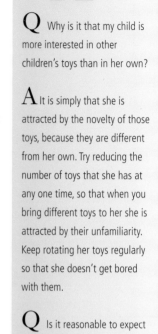

Q Why is it that my child is more interested in other children's toys than in her own?

A It is simply that she is attracted by the novelty of those toys, because they are different from her own. Try reducing the number of toys that she has at any one time, so that when you bring different toys to her she is attracted by their unfamiliarity. Keep rotating her toys regularly so that she doesn't get bored with them.

Q Is it reasonable to expect my child to recognize herself in a photograph?

A A child this age may identify herself in a photograph if she is the only person in it and if the picture is clear and large. She may smile and point to herself, or she may just stare at it and say nothing, even though she knows the picture contains her image.

Toys: jigsaws with several pieces, puzzle toys, people and animal play figures, toys cars, play-doh

Stimulating Learning: 3 to 3½ Years

The main change in your child's learning at this age is that he concentrates more efficiently on every activity, enabling him to glean as much new information as possible. He is also more confident with learning, which makes him ready and keen to acquire new concepts. Elementary counting attracts his interest, and he considers concepts such as shape and colour in more detail than before.

CAUSE AND EFFECT

Your 3-year-old may form connections between two events that occur one after the other, even though they are not linked. For instance, he may conclude that your car doesn't start because he is in a bad mood with you. You know the two are totally unconnected, but your child's lack of experience allows him to establish a cause-and-effect link in his own mind.

When you see your child make this sort of mistaken relationship between two episodes, point out to him that they are not connected but occurred one after the other by chance. Advise him that things can happen together by coincidence.

Suitable Suggestions

Young children this age are typically egocentric, in that they see the world only from their own point of view. That's why, for example, your 3-year-old demands your attention even though you are tired and have a headache – he doesn't recognize that you have needs, too. This perspective is normal for a young child, and indicates his lack of

Above: Making different shapes with modelling clay is an excellent way to get your child to think about relative size and volume.

Below: With her toy tea set your child can practise laying out the right number of place settings for her friends or toys.

maturity, not his insensitivity. But his egocentric outlook affects his learning, too.

Try this. Shape two pieces of play-doh or modelling clay into two round balls that are the same size. Place them in front of your child and ask him to agree that they are both the same size. Talk about them being the same size, for a couple of minutes. Next, in full view of your child, roll out one ball so that it is long and thin, and the other so that it is short and fat. Make sure that your child watches you do this.

Put the two new shapes side by side and ask him which one has more in it now. The chances are that he will immediately point to the long, thin shape. He does this because his

Above: At this age your child's learning depends very much on your input and he will demand a great deal of your attention.

perspective on the world is limited and he can only fixate on one dimension at a time. Try to explain that they are both the same size. Follow this procedure with other materials, such as containers with water. These activities lead him to take a broader approach to learning.

To help improve his concentration, take him shopping with you at the supermarket. Hold up a particular food can and ask your child to find one exactly like it. Do this at the top of the aisle which contains the product. Encourage him to scan each row systematically as he walks along. If you see that he rushes down the aisle, missing items as he passes, suggest he slows down. Do this three or four times during any shopping trip – it's good practice for focusing his attention. You can also ask him to identify, say, red cars when you next go out driving with him.

Q Do children this age understand about rules of behaviour?

A Yes. Your child may not like the rules that set limits on what he is allowed to do, and he may even try to break them, but he understands rules about his behaviour. Always explain a rule to your child, especially the reasoning underlying it. He learns rules quicker when they are applied consistently.

Q Is television bad for my child?

A Your child can learn a lot from short, quality television programmes that present new information in exciting and challenging ways. The danger, however, is that he may spend too much time staring aimlessly at poor quality viewing just because the television set is there in front of him. Monitor his viewing so that you are aware of his viewing patterns.

Toys: toy telephone, imitation household utensils, alphabet jigsaw, letter puzzles, soft toys, construction blocks, doll's house

❖❖❖❖❖❖❖ Top·Tips ❖❖❖❖❖❖❖

1. Show by example. Remember that your growing child learns a great deal from watching you and the way you manage situations. Explain to him why you completed something in the way you did so that he learns this strategy.

2. Counter his frustration. In his search for new learning skills, he is bound to experience frustration. In that situation, calm your child, reassure him until he is more settled, then stay with him as he tries the same activity again.

3. Play sorting games. Ask him to tell you all the things he likes to drink. If he mentions foods, not drinks, remind him that foods are not included in this group. Do the same for several other categories of objects.

4. Help him set the table. Explain to your child that he should put one knife, fork and spoon on the table for each person. He needs to think about how many people there are, and then match each set of cutlery to each individual.

5. Clap rhythms. Clap out a simple rhythm and ask your child to repeat it – for example, two quick claps followed by two slow ones. Once he is able to do this, repeat the activity using a slightly more complicated sequence.

Stimulating Learning: 3½ to 4 Years

As she approaches the end of her fourth year, your child begins to use her memory more efficiently in order to locate objects and to recall information that is important to her. A genuine understanding of numbers develops. Other pre-school skills emerge too, such as colour and shape identification; she may recognize her own name. Your child learns from playing with other children.

Suitable Suggestions

By now, she'll have had lots of experience mixing with other children, probably at nursery and at home. These social interactions boost her learning skills because she observes other children's actions and imitates some of their discovery strategies. Children also talk to one another about challenges they face – when it comes to problem-solving, they may be more creative as a group than as individuals. Your child is likely to be more enthusiastic about learning when she is in the presence of others.

You'll find that her imaginative play starts to utilize her newly acquired concepts, and this should be encouraged. For instance, she pretend-plays shops, selling goods to customers and giving them change from her toy cash register. Provide toys that stimulate this sort of imaginative play. Your child may also start to play 'schools' with her friends. She isn't sure what really goes on there, but has an idea from older siblings and television programmes.

A useful strategy for helping your child's memory is to encourage the use of rehearsal (repetition). Teach her a short poem or a telephone number. Explain that she should learn this one bit at a time. For every few words, or part of the phone number, suggest that she recites it out loud, over and over again. You intuitively use this technique when trying to commit something to

Below: You can fire your child's imagination by providing some simple dressing-up items; enthusiasm for this will be greater when he plays with his friends.

Right: More complex toys come into play at this age. This little girl is able to record her own voice and then play it back.

memory, but your child doesn't – she needs you to suggest it. Let her walk up and down the house saying the information over and over again. She'll be surprised to discover that she can easily recall it the next day, too.

There might be times when she is convinced she is right about something even though you know she is wrong. A child this age has an amazing capacity to deny reality in the face of conflicting evidence. If you find yourself trying to persuade your 4-year-old that, for example, her new jumper is red not

blue, calmly bring the jumper out to show her, patiently point out its real colour, and then change the conversation. The next time she talks about the jumper, she'll refer to it as red.

Below: By the age of 4, children are more likely to work together to solve problems – in this case a jigsaw puzzle.

✶✶✶✶✶✶ Top·Tips ✶✶✶✶✶✶

1. Encourage her to use a desk. She'll soon discover that she feels more comfortable when trying to complete a puzzle or draw a picture if she sits at a desk, with the activity placed firmly in front of her.

2. Ask her to help you solve problems. Pose everyday problems to your child. For instance, ask her to think of the best way to store all the tin cans from the supermarket in the cupboard. Encourage her to think of alternatives.

3. Allow time gaps. When your child tries to learn something new, don't allow her to persevere for hours. Instead, let her practise for a couple of minutes, then make sure she takes a long break before returning to it.

4. Increase her awareness of numbers. Point out to your child that numbers appear all around her – in shop windows, on price tags and on street signs. Ask her to identify numbers between one and nine when she sees them.

5. Make memory games more challenging. Now, when you ask her to remember the items on a tray covered with a large towel, increase the number of objects from six to a dozen (though she won't get them all right).

Q&A

Q Are some children naturally gifted and talented?

A There is no doubt that some children possess exceptional abilities in some areas of development. For example, musical ability is thought to be innate, and musically talented infants show this skill very early on, perhaps by playing tunefully with toy instruments. Yet virtually all children – including yours – can learn new skills at every age, whether they are innately talented or not.

Q Why does my 4-year-old keep asking for more toys, even though we tell her they are too expensive?

A She does this for two reasons. First, she wants more toys. Second, she assumes you are able to buy them. She hasn't yet learned that there are limits on your resources. In time she develops a more realistic outlook, but in the meantime she persists with her requests.

🧸🚚 **Toys:** toy microscope or magnifying glass, notebook and pencil, dressing-up clothes, face masks, construction set, magnetic numbers

Stimulating Learning:
4 to 4½ Years

Your child shows many of the learning characteristics that will soon help him thrive in the infant class. His awareness and understanding of numbers, shapes, sizes and time all increase, and he deals with other abstract thoughts such as comparisons. Concentration and memory also improve – he plays for longer with one toy and completes more activities instead of leaving them unfinished.

MAKING HIM THINK

Learning is not just about acquiring information but also about developing problem-solving strategies. You can extend your child's thinking skills by posing simple problems for him to solve, such as asking him what you should do if you are out in the car and it breaks down, or if you go to a shop and then discover you have no money.

As he offers his own solutions, discuss each one in detail, looking at the advantages and disadvantages. Be positive about his suggestions, even if they seem inappropriate. What matters is that your child develops strategies for reaching solutions.

Suitable Suggestions

Encourage him to take a more organized approach to learning situations: if your child chooses to draw or make a model or complete a puzzle, suggest to him that before he starts he should think about everything he could need. This might include pencils and paper, a tray or desk to lean on, a small snack, a comfortable cushion, proper lighting and the toy itself. Once he has identified the key items, tell him to arrange them in a way that suits him. Having organized himself like that, your child is now ready to begin, without having to get up unnecessarily. He concentrates better as a result, and therefore learns much more effectively.

Play lots of memory games with him. These are good fun, while also benefiting his recall skills. You could play 'When I went to the supermarket I bought a....' – each time the next person repeats what the previous players have bought and then adds a new item to the end of the list. Another suitable game is to cut out several squares each from blue, yellow and red cards, then show your child a short sequence of, say, a red, a blue and a yellow square, take it away and ask him to make the same sequence with his own cards. Vary the sequence of cards each time. Your

child will probably manage to remember three or four items accurately before becoming confused.

Below: By getting your child to predict the results of experiments like deciding what will float or sink you will help to develop his powers of reasoning.

Above: By this age your child will be intrigued by basic scientific concepts – like the fact that certain things dissolve in liquid – and will love to perform simple experiments.

To improve his performance at these games, suggest that he uses imagery. For instance, if the first colour in the sequence is red, he could imagine the front door of his house is red; and if the second colour is yellow he could imagine his hall carpet is yellow, and so on. This type of imagery helps improve his recall of the colour sequence.

Practise counting with your child, too. He can probably count to ten by rote, without missing out any of the numbers. He may also be able to count objects up to ten, perhaps counting each step as he walks slowly upstairs or counting a row of blocks in front of him, although he may miss out some. Give him number-sorting and matching activities. For instance, make a pile of four wooden blocks and ask him to make a similar pile. Vary the numbers involved each time. As well as consolidating his grasp of numbers, these games boost his confidence with learning.

You can also use learning activity books – covering topics such as numeracy and literacy – available from most quality bookshops. Do some practical science experiments with your child, such as weighing different amounts when cooking, dissolving sugar in warm water, measuring lengths of objects, using magnets – each time, ask him to predict what will happen. Explaining about growing plants in the garden also fascinates him.

✦✦✦✦✦✦✦ Top·Tips ✦✦✦✦✦✦✦

1. Give him number activities. Ask him to set the table for five people. He should count out five knives and five forks, and then set them out on the table. This type of activity relates number calculations to everyday life.

2. Explain about encyclopedias and dictionaries. When your child asks you a factual question, whether or not you know the answer, let him see you look up the information in a reference book. Tell him where to find these in your house.

3. Discuss time phases. Chat with your child about the different events that occur during his day, using time-related words such as 'morning', 'lunch' and 'afternoon' in your discussion. This reinforces his underlying concept of time.

4. Play sequence games. Draw a sequence of three actions on separate cards – for instance, a child with a full plate of food, with a half-empty plate, and with a totally clean plate. Ask your child to put these pictures in the right order.

5. Talk about similarities. To help your child's classification skills, name two or three items and ask him to say how they are the same. For instance, say 'horse', 'dog' and 'elephant' – he'll guess accurately that they are all animals.

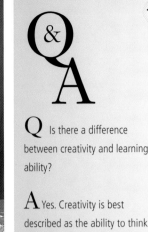

Q&A

Q Is there a difference between creativity and learning ability?

A Yes. Creativity is best described as the ability to think in new and innovative ways about old problems. A genuinely creative idea is unusual, relevant, and offers a completely new perspective. To encourage your child's creativity, let him use his imagination, show interest in his questions and give plenty of praise when he offers unusual suggestions.

Q How much detail should I give in my replies to my 4-year-old's questions? He asks lots about science.

A Reply to any questions about science in a way that is suitable for his level of understanding. Although your 4-year-old might ask what appears to be a deep question, he needs a reply that is pitched at his stage of development and understanding, without too much detail.

Toys: balancing scales, magnetic numbers and letters, plastic binoculars, toy medical kit, child's desk, alphabet wall chart

Stimulating Learning: 4½ to 5 years

In this six-month period which leads up to – and perhaps includes – your child's start in the infant class, she consolidates her existing learning skills, leaving her ready to take on the key educational challenges of reading, writing and counting. Although she is perhaps both apprehensive and excited about the prospect of the classroom, she has a positive attitude to learning.

Suitable Suggestions

Now is the time to have a long think about the main characteristics needed for your child to thrive educationally once she starts school, and then, having identified them, to

Above: Board games involving a die and simple counting will entertain your child and help his counting to become more automatic.

boost them. Take listening skills, for instance, which are important for learning in the classroom. Tell her to listen while you read a short story and add that you will ask her some questions about it afterwards. Practise this type of activity with her, gradually making both the story itself and the subsequent questions more difficult.

She is ready to play board games that involve rolling a die. Encourage her to study the die closely so that she can count the correct number of spots, then to move her piece on the board the appropriate number of squares. Be patient with her when she becomes confused, and encourage her to count again if necessary.

Left: Between the ages of 4 and 5 children are able to sort objects and group them by size, shape and colour.

Above: A garden or park offers a wealth of opportunity for your child to observe different plants and the way they change throughout the year.

Help her to be aware of her surroundings, and to scan around her as she walks along. For instance, she should notice traffic and take suitable safety precautions, she should observe the road crossing lights and she should memorize the shops along her regular route. Processing information from her everyday world sharpens her information-processing skills in general. Talk to her about the way in which weather and plants change with the seasons, and about the different people and places she sees when out walking.

She won't yet have realized that she can structure areas of her memory, just as she can, for instance, structure areas in her bedroom. Teach her this strategy as an aid to her memory. For instance, show your child a collection of nine objects – three to do with writing (pen, pencil, paper), three to do with eating (fork, cup, biscuit) and three to do with crafts (scissors, adhesive tape, glue) – mixed together. Once she has looked at them for a few seconds, ask her to remember as many as she can. Then ask her to remember the ones to do with eating. She'll find that her recall is better when she uses an orderly system to access her memory.

Below: Although your child can't yet tell the time, she is aware that her day is made up of different phases: that she has breakfast in the morning, has lunch at midday and goes to bed at night.

✦✦✦✦✦✦✦ Top ∙ Tips ✦✦✦✦✦✦✦

1. Talk positively about school. An anxious child doesn't learn as quickly as a relaxed child. Do your best to put her at ease, take her on any pre-entry visits, and tell her how much she will enjoy learning in the infant class.

2. Teach coin recognition. Pick one low-value coin and tell your child its name and how much it is worth. When she is ready, let her pick out coins of this value from a bundle you hand to her.

3. Get her familiar with computers. You may have one at home; if so, encourage your 5-year-old to become generally comfortable with the very basic uses of a computer. There are lots of child-centred CD Roms available and she'll enjoy playing with these.

4. Play matching and sorting games. Give her items which she can sort by various characteristics such as colour, shape, big and small, hot and cold, rough and smooth, loud and quiet. Then get her to sort using two characteristics – for example, putting the smooth, blue blocks together.

5. Encourage persistence. Do what you can to persuade your child to persist with a learning challenge until she achieves success. Suggest that she keeps trying for a few minutes more even though the solution eludes her at the moment.

Q My 5-year-old won't sit still. What should I do?

A Tell her gently that you expect her to sit for longer periods. Give her an interesting activity (such as colouring-in) and ask her to work at it until you tell her to stop. Finish after a minute. Give her praise for sitting there. Gradually extend the time by 15 seconds each session.

Q How can I teach my child basic number skills?

A The most effective way at this age is to teach number concepts using practical objects, such as a row of blocks spread in front of her, or her fingers. Show her that numbers correspond to objects. Then there are number songs too, such as '10 green bottles' or '5 little speckled frogs'. Make all learning activities about numbers informal, relaxed and fun.

🧸🚂 **Toys:** pencils and sharpener, child's desk, jigsaws, board games, word lotto, flashcards, toy money and cash register

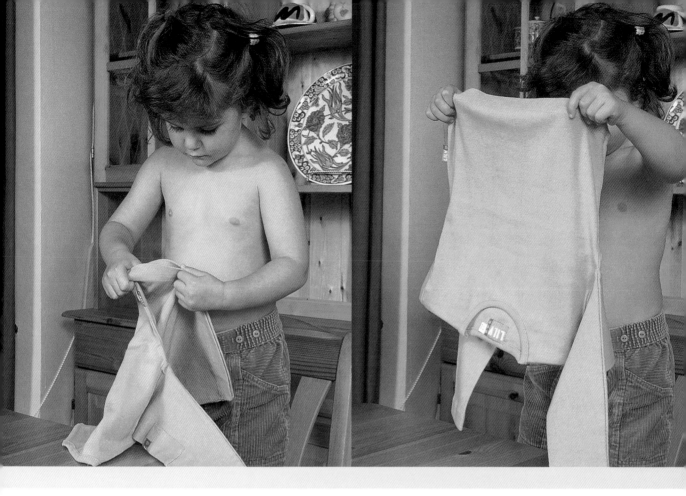

Social and

Emotional
Development

The Importance of Social and Emotional Development

The change in your child's emotional and social development during this phase of his life is remarkable. His individuality shows through in all areas, and he becomes his own person with his own characteristics, his own strengths and weaknesses, and his own relationships. No longer so dependent on you for everything, your growing child strives to manage things by himself.

Your Changing Child

Of course, these changes render him vulnerable. One minute he is very buoyant and confident in the company of other children his own age, the next he bursts into tears and then clings tightly to you; one minute he insists he doesn't need any help putting on his vest, the next he screams hysterically because his arms are entangled in the garment.

Some of the major areas of emotional and social change that your growing child experiences between the ages of 2½ and 5 years are:

• **friendships.** Your child's awareness of his peers – and his innate need to form connections with them – assumes considerable importance in his young life. He wants to be liked and to have plenty of other children with whom he can play. As he discovers, however, friendships function within a system of rules concerning sharing, supporting and turn-taking –

many of these essential social skills don't come naturally to a pre-school child. He has to learn them.

• **independence.** Not only does he want to do more for himself, he becomes increasingly capable of achieving that target. For instance, he is reliably clean and dry

during the day and he wants to achieve this control at night, too; he handles cutlery more effectively, preferring to eat alongside his family than to have meals on his own. As before, though, you may find that his aspirations outstrip his ability, and that he simply can't always manage independently.

• **gender.** His sense of 'boyness' and 'girlness' – in other words, his understanding of what makes a boy a boy and a girl a girl – strengthens. Children this age begin to drift towards same-sex friends and same-sex toys and games. Boys and girls begin to express different preferences for clothes as their gender identity develops, and they form clear ideas about appropriate behaviour for boys and girls. Gender stereotypes show through.

• **sociability.** Social situations are less challenging now as his confidence when mixing with others increases. Much of this stems from experience of

Left: Although your child increases in confidence all the time, he will need your reassurance when a situation becomes too much for him.

Above: Play fighting – and real fighting – between siblings is normal but this is a crucial age at which to establish what is acceptable behaviour and what is not.

mixing with other children and adults, whether at playgroup, nursery, in the street, out shopping with you or at family gatherings. There are continued episodes of shyness, especially when he is confronted by strangers, but he is generally more at ease in his relationships with others. He is fun to be with.

• **morality.** Your child's grasp of right and wrong goes through a noticeable transformation. He understands about lying and why he shouldn't do it (though he still resorts to this strategy at times), and he is also more aware that swearing and stealing are not acceptable. By the time he is 4 or 5 years old, your child may have very rigorous, inflexible moral principles which he expects everyone to follow. His sense of justice is also rigid. When he thinks an injustice has taken place he may be extremely upset, convinced that it needs to be righted – and he might be inconsolable until this happens.

Accepting Him

His key characteristics are evident at this age, and you'll see his nature and personality type showing through. In many ways, the challenge facing you is not to change your child's individual traits but to encourage and channel those that you admire and discourage those you do not value so highly. For instance, determination is a great asset for any child, but not when this creates distress for everyone. A child with that personal characteristic needs to be shown how to manage his determination so that it works in his favour, not against him.

This means that you should accept your child for who he is, with his own unique blend of features that make him so special. The fact is

Below: Whatever your child's personality she needs your encouragement to help her gain self-confidence and self-esteem so that she can cope with the world outside.

that changing his personality is extremely difficult, but helping him to develop particular strengths is easier. He needs your support and guidance at this stage – not criticisms or objections – to fulfil his full social and emotional potential. His basic need to be loved and valued by you remains strong; he wants your approval.

Self-Esteem

The knowledge that you think he's marvellous is one of the foundation stones on which his self-esteem and self-confidence rest. But they also depend on the reactions that he receives from other people. That's why an innocent remark from another child about his inability to run fast or his poor drawing skills throws him into emotional turmoil. He cares that others think highly of him or poorly of him; he wants to be valued.

His feeling of competence is also very important as the start of school approaches. A child who has a confident, capable frame of mind, full of self-belief about his abilities, looks forward to the infant class with great excitement. Self-doubts create the opposite effect in a child, leaving him in fear at the prospect of the classroom. Help him develop a positive attitude towards school.

Social and Emotional Development

Age	Skill
2½–3 years	Your child tries to do more for herself. Her desire for independence shows through in many areas, especially with control of her bowel and bladder during the day.
	She still has raging temper tantrums occasionally and seems to lose all control at these times. However, tantrums become less frequent towards the end of her third year.
	The company of other children matters to your growing child, though she still lacks the social skills required to take part in full cooperative play.
3–3½ years	Experience of mixing with other children and adults boosts her confidence in social situations and she is more at ease in company. She finds it easier to make new friends.
	Behaviour at mealtimes has improved vastly. She understands the social dimension of eating and she wants to be independent at the table, just like the others in her family.
	Having mastered bowel and bladder control during the day, she may also have achieved the same at night. However, some children take longer than others to reach this point.
3½–4 years	Your child has a better understanding of the social rules when playing with her pals. She is more able to share her toys, take turns in a game and follow rules.
	As her moral development is under way, she knows what it means to tell a lie. You may find, though, that she denies her misbehaviour even when you catch her red-handed.

From 2½ to 5 Years

What to Do

Encourage her to be reliably clean and dry during the day, and to manage her dress or trousers and pants when using the toilet. Look for signs that she is ready to begin night training – for instance, her nappy is dry in the morning when she wakes.

Do your best to calm her when she becomes enraged, but don't give in to her. Once she has settled down, talk to her about her tantrums. Explain that she should try harder to control her temper, and that you are upset by her tantrums.

Watch when she plays with her pals. If you see that she has difficulty with sharing – for instance, she prefers to cling to her toys rather than let anyone else get their hands on them – reassure her that the other child will return the toy to her in a few minutes.

Tell her that the children at playgroup or nursery will like her and that she will have good fun there. Let her see how pleased you are when she chats about her friendships. Ask lots of questions concerning her pals so that she can see that you are interested.

Encourage your child to use cutlery properly – probably just a fork and spoon at this age – and to sit at the table throughout the whole meal. Make sure that she has a chance to speak during the meal; she may be the youngest, but she likes to tell her news, too.

Approach night training positively – many children are still wet at night until the age of 5 years or more. Praise your child when she wakes up in the morning in a dry bed, and if the bed was wet today reassure her she'll succeed soon.

You can practise these social skills at home with your child so that she plays cooperatively with others. Play board games with your 4-year-old, encouraging her to be patient, to follow the rules and to wait her turn. Relax her if she becomes upset.

Don't over-react when your child lies to you at this age, no matter how frustrated and angry you feel with her. By all means let her see that you are displeased, but calmly explain that it's better to tell the truth than to lie. Repeat this explanation each time.

Social and Emotional Development

Age	Skill
	Her dressing skills have improved to the extent that she makes a good attempt to put on her clothes in the morning without your help. At times she gets the items mixed up, putting them on back to front or inside out, or putting her shoes on the wrong feet.
4–4½ years	She is more comfortable in the presence of familiar and unfamiliar adults, and can answer enquiries appropriately when these adults question her about herself.
	Boys tend to play with boys and girls with girls. Your child has different expectations of the way boys and girls dress, behave and play. Gender stereotypes have formed.
	More than ever before, your child judges the merits of her own abilities by comparing herself to others with whom she plays. Her self-esteem is influenced by peer comparisons.
4½–5 years	Your child shows a more caring and sensitive attitude towards others who are upset; she is genuinely troubled by their tears and does her best to make them feel better.
	Now that she is ready to start school, she takes much more responsibility for herself. However, she still needs prompts and reminders from you.
	She separates well from you when you drop her off at her childminder, nursery or playgroup. Any reluctance to separate from you is only momentary.

From 2½ to 5 Years

What to Do

Encourage her to become independent with dressing. You can help by organizing her clothes in a neat pile, with the first item on top. Suggest that she puts these on by herself, though you may need to stand beside her in order to give advice.

Encourage her to chat to visiting relatives whenever possible, so that her confidence in these situations improves steadily. Point out to your child that she should make eye contact with the person speaking to her, and that she should reply in a clear voice.

Suggest to your child that she plays with a wide range of children, both boys and girls, and that she also plays with a wide range of toys and games. If she does make statements based on gender stereotypes, explain that each boy and girl is an individual.

When she complains about her weaknesses, point out her strengths. Emphasize that nobody is good at everything and tell her that you think she is a terrific child, irrespective of how her characteristics measure up against some of the other children.

Praise your child when you see her help another child in distress. And if she doesn't know what to do to cheer up her pal, suggest she offers them a toy to play with. Her natural instinct to be kind flourishes with your interest and approval.

Put your child in charge of tidying her toys away each day and give her small areas of household responsibility, such as setting out the cutlery for the evening meal. Encourage her to complete these minor tasks of independence without seeking help.

Give her plenty of experience of temporary separations with others carers or at her friend's house. Always remind her that you'll be back to collect her very soon, give her a quick cuddle, and then leave her there. Chat to her when you do return.

Stimulating Social and Emotional Development: 2½ to 3 Years

Your child now prefers to play with his friends, rather than on his own. He doesn't yet have the ability and understanding to play cooperatively, but he does try hard – expect episodes of bickering, however. Tantrums are still present at this age, though they are usually less frequent. His desire for independence shows through, as he attempts to complete basic tasks by himself.

TELEVISION

Common sense tells you that your 3-year-old child is emotionally affected by the television and video programmes he watches. That's why you need to encourage him to watch items that are psychologically suitable for his age and understanding. Do your best to ensure that he sees only quality children's material, not violent or aggressive images that are directed at adults.

Television can be good for your child's emotional development because it can show him models of good behaviour – and it also entertains him. Problems arise, though, when a child this age watches psychologically inappropriate programmes, containing hostility and conflict.

Suitable Suggestions

Although your child likes playing with others his own age, he still experiences episodes of shyness. For instance, he might start crying as you approach the door of his playgroup or nursery, claiming that he doesn't want to go there. Don't get annoyed with him. Instead, tell him that he will have a great time, that the others really like him, and that there are lots of terrific toys. These words, coupled with a quick comforting hug, are all that he needs to help him overcome this temporary emotional hurdle.

You'll find that when he does play with his friends, there is more interaction between them than before. He talks to his friends and vice versa, and they may even play together with the same toy. But your child still has a lot to learn about social skills. Just like his pal, he may object to sharing his toys; he may prefer to snatch a toy from his friend's hand rather than ask for it. These points of minor confrontation are common at this age.

It's important, though, that your child learns from these incidents. True, you need to get involved when you see your child fighting with his friend over, say, possession of a

Below: As your child approaches 3 you will notice that there is a greater element of cooperative play with other children.

Left: Children thrive on being given small responsibilities – like tidying away some of their own toys or helping you to lay the table.

particular toy, yet try to do this positively. Show him how to share his toys and explain why he should share. Give practical reasons about the implications for him. For instance, you could tell him that he'll get invited back to his friend's house if he shares or that he benefits when his friend shares. Regularly repeat these explanations to him.

Your child's unique personality comes through now. He has discovered that he has thoughts, feeling and ideas that are different from yours, and he likes to express them to you. At this age, he expects his ideas to dominate – hence the tantrums when things don't go precisely the way he wants. When he does get angry, explain to him that his behaviour upsets you. Part of growing up involves recognition that other people have feelings too, so point this out to your child.

Below: Your enthusiasm and praise of your child reinforces her sense of self-worth: your good opinion matters greatly to her.

✧✧✧✧✧ Top·Tips ✧✧✧✧✧

1. **Help him learn to take turns.** This is an important social skill. When he's at home with you, suggest that you take the first sweet out of the bag instead of him, or that his sister should be allowed to choose the video.

2. **Tell him you like him.** He'll feel great about himself when you tell him that, for instance, he has a lovely singing voice, or that he's fun to be with. Supportive and positive comments like these reinforce his self-esteem.

3. **Give him a couple of small household tasks.** At the age of 3, he's capable of understanding and taking on small responsibilities about the house, such as putting his toys into the toy box before he goes to sleep.

4. **Expect fluctuating behaviour.** There may be frequent moments of squabbling with his pals or perhaps times when they deliberately get up to mischief together. Point out the alternative ways he could act in these situations.

5. **Provide social opportunities.** Resist any temptation to keep your child at home because he fights with other children so much – he won't learn anything with that strategy. The more he mixes with others, the more chances he has to learn.

Q&A

Q Is it normal for a 3-year-old to be unhappy at times?

A Yes, he can have moments of unhappiness, perhaps because he has lost a toy or because you have reprimanded him. However, these feelings usually pass quickly. A child may also be unhappy for more serious reasons, such as parental arguments, bereavement of a relative, sibling rivalry or poor self-esteem.

Q Sometimes my child insists on trying to do something that is much too difficult and then he has a tantrum. What should I do?

A If possible, watch your child when he tries to do something new. Should you notice him become agitated, distract his attention onto a totally different activity before he reaches explosion point. He can always come back to the original challenge later.

Toys: puzzle toys, bat and ball, dressing-up clothes, large soft ball, plastic cars, toy telephone, soft toys

Stimulating Social and Emotional Development: 3 to 3½ Years

Making new friends is the name of the game now. Your child loves mixing with others and her social skills improve significantly. These relationships with her peers boost her social confidence, making her less shy with unfamiliar children and adults. Her independence surges, especially with night-time bowel and bladder control, but also with other areas of self-care such as dressing and eating.

COMFORTERS

There are plenty of children this age who use a comforter (typically, a favourite cuddly toy) when they are tired, unwell or even just watching television quietly. The comforter helps the child relax, bringing feelings of security and contentment, and is a normal part of childhood.

Do your best to discourage her from taking the comforter with her to nursery, however, as she may be the only child there with one. If she does ask to take it, tell her to leave it behind in a safe place and that she can have it when she comes back home.

Suitable Suggestions

There is lots you can do to encourage your child's natural kindness towards others, especially now that she spends more time in the company of her peers. Point out to her that her caring actions have direct effects on others. For example, when she brings you a biscuit from the kitchen instead of just taking

Below: Remember that simply by spending time having fun with your child you are making him feel that you value and enjoy his company.

one for herself, tell her how good that made you feel. She is more likely to act kindly towards others when she realizes the impact of her caring acts. Make a big fuss of your child when you see her help her friends – your praise for that behaviour reinforces it.

This is also a good time to develop her self-help skills further. By now she has presented signs that she is ready for night toilet training (by waking in the morning with a dry nappy, by complaining during the night that her nappy needs to be changed, or even by asking you outright if she can try sleeping without a nappy). Move on to the next stage by letting her go to bed just wearing padded pants. Don't expect a dry night at first and be

prepared to change the sheets every morning for at least the first few weeks. Tell your child that you hope she will have a dry night, and add that she mustn't worry if the bed isn't dry when she wakes in the morning.

You may be lucky and find that she learns night bowel and bladder control very quickly. Most children, however, take several weeks, even months, to achieve this. Bear in mind that a child who is anxious about staying dry at night is more likely to wet herself, so everyone needs to stay calm. When anger or frustration creeps in due to lack of success, that success becomes even more elusive.

Make sure that you find time every day to spend alone with your child. Her basic need to feel valued and loved by you remains as strong as ever. Of course, relationships with peers are vital, but her basic emotional connection with you remains the cornerstone of her development.

Below: Your child will relish the sense of independence she gets from doing things for herself – like choosing her own breakfast and pouring out her own milk.

✦✦✦✦✦✦ Top·Tips ✦✦✦✦✦✦

1. Buy her a small pet to care for. She'll love having ownership of a small animal, such as a hamster or gerbil. Explain to her how to care for the animal and how to feed it, and help her to do this every day.

2. Don't let her barge into conversations. Your child slowly learns that chatting to someone involves listening as well as talking. If she does break in while you are in mid-sentence, continue talking until you have finished and then let her speak.

3. Talk about her friendships. When you are relaxing together, ask your child about her friends. Encourage her to identify the characteristics that make her like them and then talk about these. This helps her to evaluate friendships more carefully.

4. Comfort her when she cries. Despite her apparent surge in confidence, she remains fragile and emotionally vulnerable. When you see her upset over what appears to be something minor, give her a big reassuring hug to cheer her up.

5. Use non-physical forms of punishment. Smacking your child for her misbehaviour will only make matters worse. Far better to find a non-violent way of punishing her, perhaps using a verbal reprimand or sending her to her room.

Q My child still wakes up too early in the morning. What can we do?

A Tell her the night before that if she does wake up early, she should stay in her room and play quietly with her toys. Certainly, she should not come into your room at that time. Leave a pile of books and toys by her bedside so that she can reach them easily in the morning.

Q My 3-year-old talks to an imaginary friend. Does this mean she is lonely?

A No, it doesn't. Many popular children this age have an imaginary friend. Most psychologists agree that the appearance of a fantasy playmate is simply an extension of the child's imaginative ability. You'll find that her imaginary friend disappears one day, just as suddenly as it first appeared.

Toys: dressing-up clothes, animal and people play figures, toy cars, pretend cutlery and crockery, elementary board games

Stimulating Social and Emotional Development: 3½ to 4 Years

Aside from improving his social skills during this period, your child begins to understand the difference between the truth and a lie. He knows that it is wrong to lie – but he'll tell a lie at times if he thinks that is the best way to get himself out of trouble. You may find that an element of competitiveness creeps into his relationships.

TELLING LIES

Psychological research has shown that almost every child is capable of lying, if the threat of punishment for admitting the truth is very extreme. Four-year-olds do occasionally tell lies because they think this will get them out of trouble. They also tell lies for other reasons, such as to make life more interesting, to express their vivid imagination and to exaggerate their achievements. While you should deal with lies immediately they arise, don't be too harsh or your child will simply make a bigger effort to conceal the truth the next time.

Explain to your child why he should not lie (for instance, because others won't want to play with him, or because you'll be sad), and make any punishment for lying small, quick and appropriate.

Suitable Suggestions

Arguments are common among young children, and it's important for your child to learn how to handle them without resorting to aggression. His first reaction when in disagreement with one of his pals might be to become physically abusive (hitting, punching or biting) or to become verbally abusive (swearing, screaming or name-calling). Help him manage his aggression so that he resolves conflict in a less confrontational manner. Most importantly, explain to him

Below: Whatever you want to say to your child word it positively, even if you are telling her not to do something – criticism undermines her self-esteem.

that you disapprove strongly of acting aggressively towards others, that this upsets them and that other children will not play with him if they think he is aggressive.

In addition, suggest to him that he voices his feelings instead of acting on them, so that when another child snatches a toy from his hands, he might say 'I'm playing with that toy, you can have it when I've finished', instead of lashing out in anger. If that doesn't work, he should tell the nearest adult what has happened.

When you do offer guidance to your growing child, try to phrase your advice positively. A

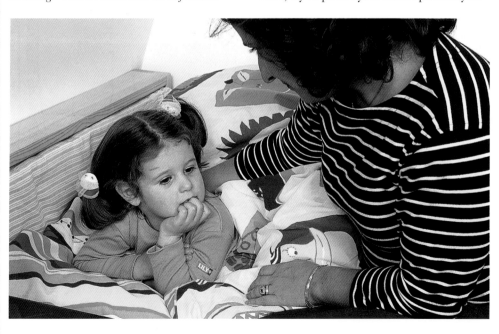

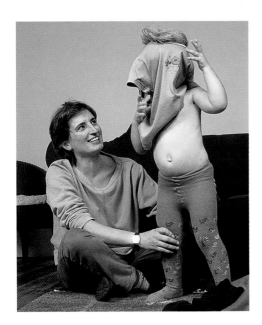

Left: Be patient while your child is learning to dress herself – if you help her too soon she may feel that you don't have confidence in her ability to do it correctly.

constant run of negative comments from you reduces his self-confidence, so find a way of expressing your ideas without leaving him to feel as though he is criticized all the time. Rules can be explained positively ('Be nice to your friends when they play with you' instead of 'Don't be horrible to your friends') and criticisms can be made without a totally negative slant ('I'm upset that you hit your pal because you're normally so friendly').

Show enthusiasm when he tries to be independent. The problem is that you can probably do things quicker yourself and your child's desire to manage on his own often slows things down. Dressing, for instance, takes much longer when he does it all by himself. That's why you need to give him plenty of time in these situations. If you know that putting on his vest and pants takes several extra minutes, make sure he starts dressing several minutes earlier than usual.

Below: Toy guns and weapons encourage aggressive behaviour among children, which may continue into other games, and so they should be avoided.

✸✸✸✸✸ Top·Tips ✸✸✸✸✸

1. Read books with sociable themes. Try to find a story book that involves children sharing their toys and playing peacefully together. He'll enjoy listening to you read it to him and the theme helps him to think about his friendships.

2. Encourage board games. Following the rules of a game can be difficult, but it is a skill that your child learns through experience. You might need to supervise him and his friends when they are playing a board game, to ensure they stick to the rules.

3. Avoid toy guns and weapons. There is evidence from research which indicates that a child who plays with an 'aggressive' toy is more likely to play aggressively with his friends immediately afterwards. Toys and behaviour are connected.

4. Reassure him when he doesn't succeed. Your child cries, for example, when he realizes he can't complete a puzzle toy that his friend manages with ease. Show him the solution and remind him of all the things he can do.

5. Praise good behaviour. It's easy to fall into the trap of focusing too much on his negative actions. Don't forget to give him lots of praise and approval when he does behave appropriately to you, his siblings and his friends.

Q Why does my child stand there saying nothing when I catch him misbehaving?

A He probably doesn't know what to say and so chooses to keep quiet. But don't let his silence stop you from talking to him. Let him know that you disapprove and give him the reasons why you are annoyed with his behaviour. He listens to you even though he doesn't say anything.

Q Should I force my shy 4-year-old to go to parties?

A Try persuasion, not force. When he receives the next invitation to a party, strongly encourage him to go. Prepare him in advance by suggesting things he can say to the other children and give him loads of reassurance, as this helps to reduce his shyness. (You could even stay with him for a couple of minutes to help him settle – the party giver's mother won't object.) And after the party, tell him how proud you are of him.

Toys: board games, construction blocks, toy farm with animals and buildings, toy musical instruments, craft materials

Stimulating Social and Emotional Development: 4 to 4½ Years

Your child's friendships are now more stable, and petty arguments during play become less frequent. She understands the need for rules, not only for play but also for her behaviour at home – she wants to please you. You find that she is more outgoing with adults who talk to her, and she is able to take part in longer conversations with you.

FEARS

Research reveals that the majority of children this age develop a fear about something; girls tend to have more fears than boys. The most common childhood fear is of small, fast-moving animals – your child may be terrified when she discovers the hamster has escaped from its cage. Some children are afraid of failure.

If your child tells you she is afraid, treat her remarks seriously. Reassure her that she has nothing to be afraid of, and hold her hand as she confronts the focus of her anxiety. Her fear subsides once she realizes that she coped better than she expected.

Suitable Suggestions

Help your child to become an independent thinker, someone who doesn't simply follow her pals aimlessly without having her own ideas. It's better if she can make up her own mind, independent of group pressure. You can develop this characteristic by involving her in minor choices, such as selecting the games she wants to play next, the jumper she would like to wear today, or the snack she would like later this afternoon. Of course this doesn't mean that you always have to agree with her choice, but at least give her the opportunity to make her own decisions.

Another technique for encouraging your child to plan is to allow more flexibility in her routine. Of course daily routines remain important to her, but if she gives you a sensible reason for organizing her schedule differently then consider her request seriously. She responds positively when you offer her more freedom with decisions.

And let her voice her opinions, even if they clash with your views. Ask her to explain why she made a particular remark or why she likes a particular television programme. Establishing a dialogue of this nature gets your 4-year-old into the habit of thinking for herself. Her confidence improves when she has a say in finding solutions to problems and

disagreements. In the long run, this makes her a more interesting, competent individual and more fun to be with.

Make sure she mixes with other children on most days, either through playgroup or nursery or through playing with them at home. Your child learns a great deal about herself, relationships and social skills just from playing with other children her own age. When she does invite friends to her

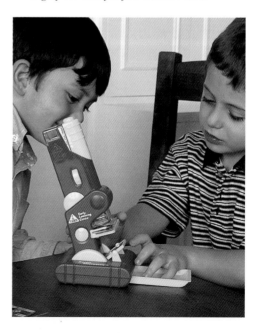

Below: By the age of 4 children have sufficient maturity to work out how to operate something and not to get frustrated if at first it doesn't work.

Right: There will now be continuity in your child's friendships as he becomes emotionally more mature and develops social skills.

house to play, speak to her beforehand, suggesting that she draws up a rough plan of activities that they can work their way through. This keeps them busy, reduces boredom and increases everyone's enjoyment.

Remember that the aim of discipline is not to control your child but to teach her a system of rules that she can apply herself. When discussing your child's behaviour with her, offer a sensible explanation for the rules you set. For instance, going to bed at a

reasonable time means that she feels good the next day, not hitting another child means that other child is unlikely to hit her, and comforting a tearful friend makes that child feel a lot better. She's old enough to understand the reasons underlying these rules and this increases the likelihood that she'll follow them.

Below: Good basic habits should now be well established and your child will understand the reasons for rules like washing his hands before meals.

✦✦✦✦✦✦✦ Top·Tips ✦✦✦✦✦✦✦

1. Practise introductions. It's always difficult for your child to know what to say when she meets another child for the first time. That's why it is useful to practise introductions at home. Teach her to say, for example, 'Hello. Would you like to play with me?'

2. Set standards for her personal hygiene. She's old enough now to take some responsibility for washing her hands and face regularly, for brushing her teeth morning and night, and for wearing fresh clothes. Check that she does this.

3. Reinforce her ambitions. If she wants, say, to be good at swimming, do what you can to arrange swimming lessons for her. This boosts her self-confidence and demonstrates that there are usually practical ways to achieve her personal aims.

4. Involve her when buying presents. It's good for your child's attitude to others to be with you when you choose a birthday card or present for someone else. Ignore any complaints of boredom and instead ask her advice when choosing.

5. Highlight strengths. It's good for your child to have spontaneous and unsolicited reminders of her positive characteristics. She'll feel so much better about herself when you mention to her, for instance, that she is interesting to talk to.

Q Is it a good idea to buy my child a pet?

A Having ownership of a small domestic pet can encourage your child's sense of caring and responsibility. Explain that she should feed the pet regularly, and make sure that she sticks to the schedule. Don't expect too much from your 4-year-old, however – for instance, she needs your help when it comes to cleaning the pet's cage or tank.

Q I don't like my child's best friend. What can I do?

A Tread carefully – you can't stop her liking another child, and if you try that may actually strengthen their relationship. The most effective technique in this situation is actively to seek out other pals for her. Arrange for her to play with lots of friends, so that she doesn't stick to one child all the time.

Toys: dice games, bat and ball, animal and people play figures, medium-sized football, skipping rope, sand tray, doll's house

Stimulating Social and Emotional Development: 4½ to 5 Years

When you look at your child's social and emotional development compared to earlier in his life, you can see how much he has matured. He is confident, has lots of friends, talks to adults comfortably and is bursting with energy and enthusiasm. The start to infant class is not far off – and he's ready for this next exciting stage in his life.

STEALING

Young children steal for a variety of reasons: for excitement, to impress their friends, to get attention from their parents, and because stealing lets them have something that they can't get by other means. Whatever the explanation, your child knows that stealing is wrong and that he shouldn't do it.

Show strong disapproval if you find he has taken one of his younger sibling's possessions. The same applies if he takes something from his friend's house or his nursery, but try to return it discreetly without drawing public attention to it. Emphasize that other children won't want to play with him if they think he is in the habit of stealing from them, and point out that there is never any justification for this sort of behaviour.

Suitable Suggestions

Aim for your child to have a successful start to school. You may be surprised to realize that the most important characteristics to enable a child to progress in the infant class are not to do with reading, counting, spelling or writing. On the contrary – the child who settles best in his class is the one with good independence and social skills.

So encourage your child to be able to look after himself. For instance, he should be able to take off his jacket and hang it on a low peg, he should be able to attend to his hygiene and dressing needs when using the toilet, and he should be able to put on his trousers and shoes after any athletic activity at school.

Think about the school experience from his point of view. Try to imagine all the social and emotional challenges facing him (such as meeting new children, or asking the teacher questions) and practise these at home with him so that he is fully confident when he steps over the threshold of the classroom. Try not to make him anxious, however. Make these activities fun.

Right: Make sure your child can manage his outdoor clothes without help and is confident about using the toilet and washing his hands on his own.

Also give your attention to the more sophisticated social skills, especially those that are required for dealing with disagreements. After all, many of your child's class assignments will involve him in group work, in which he has to listen to others and cooperate with them. He needs to be able to get on with his classmates. Advise him that when he disagrees with someone, he should express his point of view calmly, listen to the

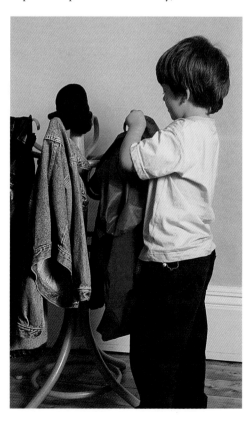

Right: Help to prepare your child for school by involving her in choosing her new bag, lunch box and things to put in them.

response and then in turn give a further reply if necessary. Conflict among children is best resolved by talking, not by yelling.

Make a point of seeking out some of the children who'll be in his class. You probably know them already because you live locally, but if you are new to the area, ask the school for advice

Q & A

Q Is this a good time to talk to my child about 'stranger danger'?

A Although you'll probably accompany him to and from school, he should be warned to be careful of strangers. In particular, tell him not to go off anywhere with a stranger or to take sweets from such a person. Tell him in such a way that he understands your message, without actually frightening him.

Q My child is nearly 5 years old but still expects me to do everything for him. How can I change this?

A Have higher expectations of your child. He has probably learned that if he stands there doing nothing, you'll eventually complete the task for him. It's time for you to stand back, do less for your child and encourage him to accept more personal responsibility.

Toys: pretend school items, board games, ball games, set of paramedic dolls, pretend post office, construction bricks

✦✦✦✦✦✦✦ Top · Tips ✦✦✦✦✦✦✦

1. Take him on a visit to his new school. Your child will lose any anxiety about starting school once he has visited it. Make sure that he sees around all the rooms, including the toilets, dining area and playground.

2. Reassure him that he'll cope. Explain that school is great fun and that he will manage all the activities in the classroom. Help him develop a positive attitude to school in order that he is enthusiastic and confident about it.

3. Teach him to be assertive, not aggressive. He needs to be able to stand up for himself, without appearing hostile. Explain that he can say 'no' to someone while still remaining calm and relaxed. Practise this with him.

4. Go out together to buy his school items. Take him with you to buy his school bag and lunch box – he probably wants to choose the ones that all his friends have. Let him also select the pencils, pencil case and crayons.

5. Believe in your child. If you have confidence in your child – if you believe he's a wonderful individual with tremendous potential – then he's more likely to believe in himself, too. And that's the best support you can give him.

on this matter. Arrange for some of these children to play with yours so that he is familiar with at least some of his classmates before the start of school.

Below: Talk to your child about school and what she will be doing there – this is an important new stage for her and if you are positive about it she will be, too.

Index of Age Groups

General Index

Acknowledgements

Executive Editor – Jane McIntosh
Editor – Sharon Ashman
Executive Art Editor – Leigh Jones
Designer – Tony Truscott
Photography – Peter Pugh-Cook
Stylist – Aruna Mathur
Production Controller – Lucy Woodhead

The publisher would like to thank all the children and parents who took part in
the photoshoot for this book for their time, energy, patience and cooperation.
We would also like to thank the following organizations for allowing us to use
their products:

Ikea, 255 North Circular Road, London NW10 0JQ Tel: 020 8233 2300 for the use of:
Bofink Chairs pink and blue *ref no.* 15684326/25684340; Måne Rocker *ref no.* 35683420;
Groda Bean Bag Cover *ref no.* 90025082; Pasig Bean Bag *ref no.* 00015742;
Lysboj Table Lamp *ref no.* 70019831; Kritter Chairs red and green
ref no. 10011178/90011179; Kritter Table *ref no.* 20011173; Fä Pelican *ref no.* 30020006;
Vikare Bed *ref no.* 55605006; Täcka Throw *ref no.* 60024404; Fruklig Quilt Cover
ref no. 60028020

Modus Publicity, 10–12 Heddon Street, London W1R 1DN

The Early Learning Centre, South Marston Park, Swindon, SN3 4TJ Tel: 01793 831300

First published in Great Britain in 2001 by Hamlyn,
a division of Octopus Publishing Group Ltd,
2–4 Heron Quays, London E14 4JP

Copyright © Octopus Publishing Group Ltd 2001
ISBN 0 600 60070 X

A catalogue record for this book is available from
the British Library

Produced by Toppan Printing Company Ltd
Printed in China